In the same
**INTERNATIONAL
FILM GUIDE SERIES**
edited by Peter Cowie

The Cinema of Orson Welles *by Peter Cowie*

Hitchcock's Films *by Robin Wood*

The Marx Brothers
Their World of Comedy *by Allen Eyles*

French Cinema since 1946
Vol. 1: The Great Tradition
Vol. 2: The Personal Style *by Roy Armes*

Swedish Cinema *by Peter Cowie*

The Musical Film *by Douglas McVay*

Buster Keaton *by J.-P. Lebel*

Animation in the Cinema *by Ralph Stephenson*

The Horror Film *by Ivan Butler*

The Western
An Illustrated Guide *by Allen Eyles*

THE CINEMA OF
JOSEPH LOSEY

James Leahy

A. ZWEMMER LIMITED, LONDON

A. S. BARNES & CO., NEW YORK

This Book is dedicated to my Father (†) and Mother.

Cover stills: front, Joseph Losey at the time of making THE SER-VANT; back (top) Dirk Bogarde (left) and Losey (right) during shooting of THE SERVANT, and (below) Jeanne Moreau (left) with Stanley Baker (right) from EVE.

FIRST PUBLISHED 1967

Copyright © 1967 by James Leahy

Library of Congress Card No. 67-22884

This edition prepared by The Tantivy Press

in association with A. Zwemmer Ltd.

and A. S. Barnes & Co. Inc.

Printed in Holland by Drukkerijen vh Ellerman Harms nv, Amsterdam

Acknowledgements

STILLS were provided and are reproduced by courtesy of the following: Alliance International and London Independent Producers *(Accident)*; Twentieth Century-Fox *(Modesty Blaise)*; Warner-Pathe *(The Servant* and *King and Country)*; Columbia *(The Damned)*; Times Film Corporation, New York *(Eve)*; Anglo-Amalgamated *(The Criminal* and *The Intimate Stranger)*; Rank *(Blind Date* and *The Gypsy and the Gentleman)*; Paramount *(The Dividing Line)*; all other illustrations, and certain stills from *The Damned*, were provided by the National Film Archive, and are reproduced by courtesy of Kingston Film Distributors *(The Boy With Green Hair)*; United Artists *(The Prowler, The Big Night)*; Columbia *(M)*; Anglo-Amalgamated *(The Sleeping Tiger)*; Eros Films Ltd. *(Time Without Pity)*. I am also extremely grateful to Rank for the loan of a print of *The Gypsy and the Gentleman*, and to Cross-Channel Films for the loan of a print of *The Intimate Stranger*, and to several people in the Education Department of the British Film Institute, particularly Sue Bennett, for helping me to screen these two films, and to the Cinémathèque Française for making the script of *Eve* available to Terry Watkins.

I am indebted to Barbara Finkelman, who typed the manuscript; to Gaila Jonaitis and Robin and Aline Wood for general encouragement with this project; to Peter von Bagh for permission to draw on his taped interview with Joseph Losey, and for many extremely valuable insights into Losey's art; to Charles Barr for not writing this book; to Terry Watkins for persuading him not to write this book, for her research in Paris, for her general assistance and encouragement, and for helping me to see the English class structure through the eyes of an American.

Finally, I should like to thank many people connected with the shooting of *Accident*, particularly Maureen Gregson and Theo Cowan, who were in charge of publicity, and Stanley Baker, also Philippa Drummond, Losey's secretary. Also Gary Dartnell, of Dartnell Films, who handles *Accident* in the U.S.A. My greatest debt, though, is to Joseph Losey himself, who did everything he could to help me with the preparation of this book, and who gave up several hours, when he was working at great pressure, to talk about his films.

Preface

This book pre-supposes rather considerable knowledge of films in general and of my films in particular. It consists partly of interviews with me (most of which were given under the pressure of work on *Accident*), partly of other earlier interviews with various people, and the author's opinions and points of view as well as those of certain other critics.

The interviews are accurate and for the most part they reflect remarkably well my basic attitudes, but this method of constructing a book necessarily results in large gaps and omissions and some wrong emphases. I am concerned about this hazard particularly with regard to my collaborators and colleagues. For instance, I believe I have mentioned only two writers who have worked with me, Harold Pinter and George Tabori; and I also seem (not altogether intentionally) to have lumped screenwriters into two categories: those who are contributive in every way, not just dialogue but structure, evocation of image and rhythm, and those who are basically "journeymen", those who are good at their craft but whose contribution does not usually extend much beyond that. If I were here to list all the writers and technician co-workers who have been omitted from this book, I might well still be slighting a number of people whose contributions have been enormous and certainly contributive. At the risk of this, I want nevertheless to give brief thanks to a number of people:

Evan Jones and Ben Barzman have certainly been highly contributive writers to the many films they have each shared with me; and Daniel Mainwaring (Geoffrey Homes) and Alun Owen on the single but crucial films they each shared with me. I wish particularly to acknowledge the contributions made in the visual

7

planning of my pictures by John Hubley and Richard MacDonald. Of the many technicians who have given their flesh and blood to help make the films what they are, I wish to make special mention of Pamela Davies whose dedication as well as her work have made such an enormous difference to my English pictures, and to the editors Reginald Mills and Reginald Beck. Of the actors in particular Dirk Bogarde, Stanley Baker, Hardy Kruger and Alexander Knox. It would be difficult to single out any of the many others to whom I owe great debts. I am grateful for the enormous personal and professional assistance given me by Norman Priggen as co-producer on my last five English pictures. Without these people I shall not say the films could not have been made. I think indeed they probably would have been, but they would have been quite different films.

To young James Leahy I am obliged for his interest and his scholarly care. As for his opinions — some of them I share, others I would strongly disagree with, and some I must confess I do not understand. It is nonetheless gratifying to be the recipient of such interest and perhaps to reach readers who may be part of the core of a new film-going audience.

London, June 1967. **Joseph Losey**

Contents

	Page
INTRODUCTION	11
1 THE CINEMA OF JOSEPH LOSEY	13
2 THE BOY WITH GREEN HAIR	28
3 THE LAWLESS	34
4 THE PROWLER	40
5 M	47
6 THE BIG NIGHT	52
7 STRANGER ON THE PROWL	55
8 THE SLEEPING TIGER	60
9 THE INTIMATE STRANGER	66
10 TIME WITHOUT PITY	69
11 THE GYPSY AND THE GENTLEMAN	74
12 BLIND DATE	79
13 THE CRIMINAL	89
14 THE DAMNED	97
15 EVE	106
16 THE SERVANT	126
17 KING AND COUNTRY	134
18 MODESTY BLAISE	148
19 ACCIDENT	156
FILMOGRAPHY	164
SELECTED BIBLIOGRAPHY	173

Key to Interviews

J.D.L.   indicates the interview granted to the author by Joseph Losey in August 1966, during the shooting of *Accident*.

I.S.   refers to the issue of the Oxford magazine *Isis* devoted to *The Servant* (1st February, 1964); this extremely important document, containing interviews with Losey, Harold Pinter, Richard MacDonald, Douglas Slocombe, Reginald Mills, John Dankworth, Dirk Bogarde, Wendy Craig, Sarah Miles, James Fox, gives some insight into the combination of free collaboration and directorial control which go to make up a Losey movie.

P.v.B.   refers to the interview granted to Peter von Bagh, and another interviewer, in April 1965, after Losey had viewed the two hour twenty minute print of *Eve* (with original soundtrack).

E.   *The Individual Eye* by Joseph Losey, *Encore*, March-April, 1961 (first published in the special Brecht issue of *Cahiers du Cinéma*, December 1960.)

C.L.   *Joseph Losey*, by Christian Ledieu, in the *Cinéma d'Aujourd'hui* series; the actual words used are: "C'est l'histoire d'Eva et de Tyvian, significative d'une certaine conception de l'hétérosexualité et du couple" in the first passage referred to; in the second passage: "*Eva* ne leur donne aucun soulagement, si ce n'est qu'en le regardant dans une optique différente, ils pourraient y trouver une délivrance par l'esthétique. Pour moi, en tout cas, c'est certain: il y a une délivrance par l'intellect, mais non par l'émotion."

S.B.   Interview granted to the author by Stanley Baker during August 1966.

F.C.   *Notes on an Early Losey* by T. J. Ross, in *Film Culture*, Spring 1966, the best piece of Losey criticism by an American writter that I know.

J.B.   *Joseph Losey and The Servant*, a conversation between Losey and Jacques Brunius in *Film 38*.

G.O.O.   Losey, interviewed by Ian Cameron, Mark Shivas and V. F. Perkins in the joint issue of *Granta* (Cambridge) and *Oxford Opinion*.

"I LIKE theatre, I like films, these two things are my life, and almost entirely my life, and they are so concentrated and involved that they very often seriously interfere with, if not exclude, private life; but they also make private life possible. But nothing could be worth the anguish and the hard work and the distress of work in these mediums that are combinations of the commercial and the free unless you are dealing successfully enough with problems to disturb people. And this again comes back to that hideous business which has been a kind of byword of film finance and film distribution and exhibition: 'It's entertainment,' or 'Is it entertainment?' or 'It's not entertainment.' What is entertainment? Entertainment, to me, is anything that is so engrossing, so involves an audience singly or *en masse* that their lives for that moment are totally arrested, and they are made to think and feel in areas and categories and intensities which aren't part of their normal life. And anything that can arrest me to that degree — whether it's music, painting, a human being, a landscape, the sensation of being alive in various ways — is entertainment, is something that lifts life a little bit out of its rut into some other category, temporarily or permanently a little bit further. But entertainment simply for the sake of oblivion is like all the other ways of getting through life and wasting time. What's the horrible phrase everybody uses? Killing time, killing time, as if time were there to be killed, which it isn't."   *Joseph Losey* (J.D.L.)

"I don't regard my work as being particularly pessimistic because I think pessimism is an attitude that sees no hope in human beings or life in general, that has no compassion therefore; and to have compassion, I strongly believe you have to examine the worst, the most tragic, the most crucifying aspects of life as well as the beautiful ones, and also the things that corrupt life, distort it, destroy it."   *Joseph Losey* (J.D.L.)

Losey's attitude is very close to that of Thomas Hardy, who is with Conrad one of Losey's two favourite English writers. Hardy wrote of himself as one:

"Who holds that if way to the better there be,
it exacts a full look at the Worst,
Who feels that delight is a delicate growth cramped
by crookedness, custom and fear."[1]

[1] Thomas Hardy: *In Tenebris II.*

12

1. The Cinema of Joseph Losey

EARLY in *The Lawless*, there is a shot of the wealthy young American boy, Joe, one of the troublemakers who precipitate the action of the film, taking a shower: he is seen through the shower curtain, back lit so as to be in silhouette. Visually this shot is strikingly similar to a rather more grotesque shot of Tony during the "cat and rat" game towards the end of *The Servant*. Losey's comment that the action of *The Servant* exposes Tony's "own lack of any purpose and credo, and his own fantasy world," his "false values" (J.D.L.) has great force when applied to Joe, Tony's American counterpart. Yet the origins of the shot in the later film have been recorded in detail by James Fox (who played Tony): "That's a great shot, I think. Joe's very good at using things like that, I mean it was quite an unscripted shot because it was unscripted that I was behind the shower curtain. I was meant to be hiding somewhere upstairs, but then we worked it out and I got in the bath; then Dougy was fooling around with the lighting, and with back lighting you got this extraordinary effect. Then of course we used it, but until then he hadn't thought of it. We were always seizing opportunities at left, right and centre." (I.S.; "Dougy" is Douglas Slocombe, the director of photography).

Whoever thought of or created the image, it was Losey's decision to use it: it is in the film because Losey's innate visual sense told him it was right. Though there was obviously no conscious intention on Losey's part, the critic cannot help but sense some kind of unconscious link between the two shots in the total context of Losey's work. And Losey's films, whatever they may owe to the creativity of others, are essentially Losey's works, expressions of a unified personal vision, though one that has evolved and developed over the years. Admittedly Losey looks upon the making of a film as a truly collaborative effort, but there is no doubt about

13

who provides the guiding creative force: "I believe that everybody should make his particular contribution: the designer, the writer, the composer, the cameraman. Everyone must be free and encouraged to make their own contribution within an overall framework and control and discipline which obviously comes from the director. And I also, for that reason, believe in teams, because the more one works with people the more one establishes an artistic language, and the more one can deepen one's work . . .

"There are in general two kinds of writers who work on films as far as I'm concerned. One who is very personal and contributive, like Pinter for instance, Pinter and George Tabori, and others who are very . . . not uncreative and not uncontributive, but who work to specific directions and ideas from the beginning to the end, and who never make the same creative contribution that a man like Pinter does. But it's very, very hard. I don't know of more than half a dozen people, anywhere, who can help me very much with a script, and I don't wish to write a script myself because then I think the film is limited, because I'm not a writer. You know, I can't. In this film *Eve*, for instance, I would say, almost without exception, practically every idea is mine. Some of the dialogue is mine, but the writer nevertheless made a contribution, and a big contribution, and if I'd tried to write that myself, I think it would have suffered. Maybe I'm wrong. Maybe I'm just lazy!" (P.v.B.)

Joseph Losey is a man of the cinema; he expresses himself through his art: "I cannot really be articulate about what I'm trying to do because I don't really know what I'm trying to do until after I've done it, and sometimes not then. And if you're dealing with a visual medium, well, if you're dealing with cinema, or if you're a painter or a musician, it's very seldom that a work which is really successful is one about which you can be fully articulate, as what you're doing is being articulate through *it*, and not through words. If you're being articulate through words,

14

you'd be a writer, presumably, or a poet." Unlike so many of his characters, Losey is lucid and has a purpose in life, a purpose intimately connected with this lucidity. His camera is its agent, linking, connecting, revealing, always at the service of his ideas, ideas which he can only make fully articulate through his camera. The sculptress Freya, in *The Damned*, when questioned about her works, says: "If I could explain these, I wouldn't have to make them." His films are manifestations of the kind of self-awareness, self-expression and freedom that his characters lack, yet they are full of characters who cannot achieve lucidity. Even the artist is not totally free: he is deeply affected by his own sometimes limiting environment and experience: one remembers the obsession of the young painter in *Blind Date*, Jan van Rooyen, with the mining community from which he comes; he finds it hard to paint beauty. Similarly in *The Damned*, Freya's works, like those of Losey himself, reflect the violence of the age in which she lives: she might be accused of an obsession with violence, as, of course, Losey has been, unjustly, I think. There is an echo of Marx here: "It is not the consciousness of men that determines their being, but, on the contrary, their social being determines their consciousness."[2] Yet Losey has written of Brecht, an artist whom he knew well, and with whom he is consequently frequently linked, perhaps too frequently and too naïvely (Losey feels that, as men of the same day and age, their relationship did not involve any simple, one way influence; often, for example, they had reached similar attitudes quite independently; he writes of "The Living Newspaper", which he helped create in New York: "This was Brechtian theatre but I didn't know it."): "Brecht well knew as he wrote in *Galileo* that 'there is no such thing as a book only one man can write.' Or play or theatre: And yet he knew quite as well (also clear in *Galileo*) of the critical difference one man of genius can make to

[2] Karl Marx: preface to *The Critique of Political Economy*.

the tempo of development and the particular character of one time and place in space." (E.). The effect of art can be liberating, therapeutic, helping to change the spectator's consciousness, because it is part of the spectator's social existence. The artist, by giving expression to his own consciousness, making articulate his own most intense concerns as a man of his day and his society, speaks for his fellow men, for his generation, perhaps for all men. In *Eve*, Billie Holiday speaks for Eve, makes articulate that despair which Eve's protective shell does not allow her to admit to herself. It was part of Losey's original conception that Miles Davis should speak in the same way for Tyvian, whose self-pitying, guilt-laden attempts at confession represent weakness rather than awareness or articulateness. Francesca, seeking spiritual certainty in a bleak universe, reads T. S. Eliot, a poet who, in his way, has often sung of "loveless love", a central theme of the film. In *The Servant*, there is a particularly touching moment during the quarrel in the restaurant with Susan, when Tony momentarily breaks down: a prisoner of illusions, he has nothing, no awareness within himself which might enable him to achieve lucidity, and thus freedom. Hamp, in *King and Country*, relies on his mouthpiece, Captain Hargreaves, with pathetic, dog-like devotion: whilst being questioned at his court-martial, he answers one of Hargreaves's questions: "Like you told me to say, I was acting under extraordinary strain." At the close of *M*, the child-murderer pours out a weird, incoherent stream of words in his defence: "A mixture of all the elements that he only half understands that went into making him what he was, and this is true of most of these characters. It's true of the inarticulateness of Tyvian." (J.D.L.). Losey feels "that most of the things that are worth saying about people are not usually the things that they can be articulate about themselves, which is one of the reasons that I usually disapprove of trying to talk at any great length about my work." (J.D.L.). However, the conditions

THE BOY WITH GREEN HAIR: Peter (Dean Stockwell) and the war orphans. Peter learns "that war is very bad for children."

THE LAWLESS: "Looks like some us have forgotten how to be men." Mr. Jensen (William Edmunds) and his sympathisers.

THE LAWLESS:
"Sometimes very tolerant . . .",
Lopo Chavez (Maurice Jara) and Paul Rodriguez (Lalo Rios) in their first encounter with the police (top) and: ". . . sometimes a lynch mob" (below)

of the art-form and the intellectual climate of the society in which Losey works have forced him into making verbal articulations, articulations that are clear, concise and meaningful, providing genuine insights into his work, though obviously lacking the polish, order, discipline and formal beauty of his works. The majority of critics see their task as consisting of making evaluative judgments, usually at the expense of the work before them, rather than attempting the more difficult, though more rewarding, job of elucidation, building a bridge of understanding, knowledge, insight and sympathy between artist and audience: "Among the other things that could be said about *Eve*, for instance, is that I am quite sure that if the Paris reception of *Eve*, in its original showing in Paris, by the critics and by an incredibly vulgar and brutal opening-night audience that came neither to see it and listen, nor to accept, but simply to attack, and to see each other, if that reception had been different, then I'm quite sure that the Hakims and all the others, whose interest in film-making is purely the gambler's interest in big money, would probably have handled it differently, and it would have had a different life and a different meaning, so I consider the critics and that audience as responsible as anybody else." (J.D.L.). The audience Losey describes seems to have inherited certain behaviour-patterns from the audience that, a hundred or so years ago, used to attend the Paris Opéra. The financial power, and commitments, of producers and distributors make a film particularly vulnerable to a hostile reception. When an opera or play is cut, the lines or music still exist, and can be reconstructed for a subsequent production. Scenes from a film are usually destroyed, and lost forever. To assess the effect of this disaster on Losey's art, one can try speculating how long it would have taken Antonioni's career to recover if the boos at the 1960 Cannes Film Festival had led to the mutilation of *L'Avventura*. The destruction of *Eve* is obviously one of the tragedies of Losey's life; he admits:

"I suppose it will remain an obsession for all my life."

In the absence of good, or responsible, criticism, Losey has found talking about his films "necessary to develop a new audience, to develop a serious audience, an audience that can begin to extend its effect even to mass distribution and mass audiences. And I think standards have changed enormously in the past ten years. To some extent, they're now even reaching producers and distributors, but certainly reaching audiences. To a lesser degree, it's reaching critics, but I think critics remain pretty well stuck in their grooves of self and egocentric satisfactions, rather than undertaking serious examinations of works, though the form that groove takes may change." Perhaps the Paris audience and critics would now respond enthusiastically to *Eve*, but Dreyer's *Gertrud* received a pretty hostile first night reception: the form of the groove has changed. However, Losey's confidence is justified; audiences now are much more aware than they were.

When interviewed, Losey time and again expresses what one had felt to be the thematic core or central concern of the film under discussion, a core that the better critics had talked round without ever quite expressing, and one which the majority of critics had ignored altogether. Perhaps, however, Losey's most consistent statement of his methods of creation can be found in an article from which I have already quoted, where he is concerned less with his own work *per se* than with his relationship with Bertolt Brecht. Losey lists, in a passage which, I feel, deserves extended discussion: "the particular aspects of Brechtian theatre and Brecht the man as I knew him that might relate to film and which have influenced my work in cinema." (E.).

First, Losey cites: "The stripping of reality and its precise reconstruction through selection of reality symbols." *(op. cit.)* Earlier in the article, he has observed that Brecht's plays "observe nature but do not reproduce it"; like Brecht, he rejects a naturalistic depiction of real life, preferring, rather, to show what life is really like, its bared, heightened conflicts. (In this, he reminds one, too, of Strindberg, whose play *The Father* Losey at one time wanted to film.) Losey does not set out to depict reality, rather he distils it — selecting the significant detail, the significant gesture, ignoring the rest. Despite a minutely observed naturalistic surface, Losey's films are essentially and clearly allegories or fables. Yvor Winters (in his book *Maule's Curse)* suggests that the Puritan division of mankind "into two groups, the saved and the damned . . . in itself represents a long step toward the allegorization of experience", and discusses this as a background to the novels of a New England artist such as Hawthorne. Films such as *The Prowler* and *The Servant* are clearly allegories; their essential structure reminds one forcibly of, say, Hawthorne's *The Scarlet Letter*. Works like *The Criminal, The Damned, Eve* are similarly allegories, though perhaps less obviously so. It is this use of allegory that makes American literature (at least that of the 19th century) in some ways strangely closer to German literature than to English literature. Interestingly enough, the film *The Servant* seems most closely to resemble is Murnau's *The Last Laugh:* in each case, the protagonist's world is destroyed because he has a dreamlike or unreal conception of reality. When his dream is shattered by the conflicts of the real world (which are, in both films, expressed principally in terms of the opposition of master and slave), he is unable to come to terms with the real world through his own efforts. Certainly Losey, though a mid-Westerner, does seem to belong in the New England Puritan tradition, which may be one reason why he found Hollywood, with its projection of the American pioneer/frontier hero image, so uncongenial. There is, too, in Losey's essentially agnostic work, in films like *The Gypsy and the Gentleman* and *Eve*, perhaps less so in *The Damned* and *The Servant*, a very definite survival of the essential paradox of Puritan theology, the struggle to accommodate a belief in both free-will and pre-destination. Losey himself says: "I certainly believe very strongly that human beings are able to shape their own destiny, and that they usually get what they deserve, and even ask for it, but I am also somewhat fatalistic, and believe in and have a sense of overall destiny." (J.D.L.)

Next in his article on Brecht Losey refers to: "The importance of precision in gesture and texture and line in objects." One has only to listen to Losey's collaborators to learn how essential a part of his art this precision is: on *Accident*, the change from black and white (in which the film was originally conceived) to colour, and Losey's growing preoccupation with the uses to which he might put colour (which derived from his pleasure with the results that were achieved with the colour from the first days of shooting on-wards) meant that some aspects of the visual style of the film changed and evolved during shooting: things that seemed right when a scene was first planned no longer looked right when it came to be shot, and "It's no good trying to get Joe to use some-thing that isn't exactly what he wants" I overheard someone say on the set, when discussing some of the ways the film had changed, and the problems that these changes involved. Losey states that, in Brechtian production, "The selected reality symbol must be perfect." *(op. cit.)*. It is this desire for the precise visual image that determines Losey's attitude towards filming in colour: "Pre-viously I've always abhorred it, because it is usually picture postcard and it certainly hasn't been controllable, either in terms of stock, light-ing conditions, processing, lab technicians, and finally prints – up till now. However my experience on the film that I'm currently working on *(Accident)* has been such a delight in terms of colour, the results I'm getting are precisely what I want, and, with the exception of perhaps two or three shots out of something like three hundred and fifty set-ups, there is nothing that isn't sheer pleasure.

So that, though this film was conceived as a black and white film, and I didn't want colour, and it was insisted on by finance, I can now no longer think of this film as having been possible in anything but colour. If I could be sure of getting colour like this, and if the colour continues to be controllable, for a lot of reasons (but the chief one in this case is the cameraman, and by the way it's his first picture as a lighting-cameraman) then I think that I would like to make every picture in colour, but I'm still worried about what will happen to the prints when it comes to putting them out in mass quantities, and I'm also worried about what will happen with all the various people who say: 'It's too dark for a smoke-filled theatre', or 'It's too low key for television,' or 'It isn't colour', or whatever"; and towards the various screen ratios: "I have worked in cinemascope twice, and found it stimulating, and like it sometimes. I like it better in black and white than I do in colour, although I have worked in both. I think standard wide-screen is a perfectly decent shape, but the trouble is that there really isn't any standard. There are two or three different ratios, and it isn't standardised, and it also is further qualified by the fact that everybody's looking for television sale, and no ratio, no present screen-ratio, can be fitted to any television screen ... Aesthetically television is absolutely destructive to serious film-making." These two references to the role television is coming to play in the financial structure of the film industry make clear the existence of what may well turn out to be a new threat to the creative independence of Losey, and other film-makers in his position. In the *New York Times* of October 30, 1966, producer Martin Ransohoff is quoted as saying: "Producers have always looked upon TV revenues as just a few bucks at the end of the line. Now all that is over. A good movie can now yield, from TV alone, an amount equal to at least half its basic cost. That spells revolutionary changes for the industry."

In the article in *Encore* which is under discussion, Losey goes on to refer to: "The economy of movement, of actors, of camera — never to move excepting with purpose"; Losey's camera is at the service of his ideas. A line or so later, Losey writes about: "The focussing of the eye through the exact use of the camera, lens and movement"; towards the end of this key passage, he emphasises: "The importance of the exact word, sound, music." The opening shot of *Eve* — one of the most beautiful fluid camera movements in Losey's, or anybody else's art — reveals Losey's central concern ("It is the story of Eve and Tyvian, signifying a certain conception of heterosexuality and the couple" (C.L.)): Venice, Tyvian's "Babylon", its statuary: the tree of life, whose leaves conceal the genitals of Adam and Eve, whose branches link the genitals of Adam and Eve: shame — which is destructive — and the creative force of sex, fused in one beautifully meaningful image of contradiction, whilst, on the soundtrack: "The man and the woman were naked together, and unashamed."

This juxtaposition of image and sound leads one on to the next Brechtian principle Losey refers to: "The juxtaposing of contrasts and contradiction through editing and in text — this is the simplest way to accomplish the much misunderstood 'alienation effect'." A page or so earlier, Losey has mentioned the Hegelian legend "Die Wahrheit ist Konkret" which Brecht had tacked above his desk in New York: "I took it to mean to Brecht not that truth was absolute, but that it was precise." In *The Lawless*, there is an incident of great complexity: after the arrest of the Mexican boy, Paul Rodriguez, Jan Dawson, a woman reporter who has been chatting about her life to the newspaper proprietor, Larry, leaves his office to 'phone in her report. As she passes the boy's worried mother in the corridor, she stops to say: "I know how you feel, Mrs. Rodriguez. I'm a mother myself." A few moments later, we hear her 'phoning through her story: "Rodriguez stood there.

Mud-covered. Sullen. Cruel. A trapped animal if ever I saw one . . . I looked for some sign of remorse; all I could see was cruelty." Similarly, the sadistic behaviour of Barrows, the chief-warden in *The Criminal*, is established in a series of incidents; during Sunday morning mass, when Bannion is plotting his escape with Frank Saffron, Losey cuts away to a medium shot of Barrows, for whom the mass is an experience of profound, orgasmic intensity, a shot which is deeply disturbing precisely because it is so strangely beautiful. Losey's montage (or editing) is an integral part of his overall dramatic conception. Some of the power of this particular shot derives as much from its relationship to the shots immediately preceding it as it does from its relationship to what we already know of Barrows' character. However, there is none of the over-literary subservience to the concept of montage as the foundation of film-art (a subservience which had its roots in false analogies with prose-writing, linked with an effort to renounce theatrical method) that one finds in the theory and much of the practice of the classic Russian directors Eisenstein and Pudovkin, where the "soulless" individual shots were, ideally, to be treated as so many pictographs in a new and very expensive kind of hieroglyphic script. Losey's shots are never "soulless", and his montage is not the kind that cuts from an important and complex historical figure to a peacock spreading its tail-feathers in the belief that a profound comment on human psychology and political behaviour is thus being made. His minutely accurate depiction of the complexity and contradictory nature of human behaviour reveals a deep antipathy to any oversimplified labelling — this man is a sadist, that one a homosexual, and so on: the truth is seldom so simple.

This rejection of the easy truth, the simple answer, is a thread that runs through the totality of Losey's work: it is as if he were continually testing and re-testing certain attitudes to life (it is perhaps this aspect of Conrad's art that makes *Nostromo* so attractive to Losey). Thus, an essential emphasis in *The Criminal* and more particularly in *The Damned* is on the destruction of innocence, and its relationship to the corrupting effect of society on the individual: "Shades of the prison house begin to close/Upon the growing Boy" — it is a notion deriving from Romanticism, Rousseau's theories of education. Tony, in *The Servant*, is a romantic, too, but one for whom the romanticism of far-away places is a form of self-evasion and escape, not a source of inspiration and strength; his romantic illusions, being a poor substitute for self-awareness, analysis of oneself and one's society, help to destroy him. Similarly, one feels that the repeated references to Gabriel's mother-fixation in *Modesty Blaise* imply a comment on certain somewhat over-glib psychoanalytical explanations of human behaviour which represent yet another over-simplification of the truth. Certainly there is a thread of psycho-analytical insight running through Losey's work — the child-murderer in *M* has a mother-fixation (a poster on the wall: "Did you write to your mother?" is a reminder of the general American obsession with motherhood — an obsession which perhaps has its origins in the fact that the population of the United States is essentially an immigrant population, lacking social cohesion), and the film, like *The Boy with Green Hair*, is full of extraordinarily beautiful Freudian symbols and references. The young criminal in *The Sleeping Tiger* is cured by the psychiatrist who, whilst permissive, encourages him to examine the nature of his "acting out"; conversely, Tony, in *The Servant*, is destroyed partly because he is allowed to act out without check or question. These psycho-analytical references are never presented as explanations of the film; they are just part of the complex totality Losey presents.

Losey's art, as has been suggested, belongs to the American Puritan tradition. A comment on Brecht reveals something about what Puritanism means to Losey: "He had the drive of a Puritan without the self-penalising guilt. (How he escaped the latter I will never know.)" *(op. cit.)* Man's struggle with and often defeat by guilt is one of the basic themes of Losey's art; guilt, and the compulsive behaviour patterns it imposes on the individual, is a denial of free-will. In *Blind Date*, Morgan's Welsh Puritanism is a positive force; it is connected with his strength and his honesty, his passionate desire for truth. Yet Morgan reveals a curious kind of sexual obsession: his voice takes on a special tone of bitterness as he refers to Jacqueline Cousteau as the kind of woman "that can drive a man half out of his senses"; he reveals an almost warped fascination (expressed in terms of an intense distaste) with the kind of sex that a call-girl represents. In *Eve*, Tyvian's Welsh Puritanism is the background that he trades on, that he hates, that he claims to have put behind him long ago, but which, in fact, still dominates him; it is intimately connected with his sexual guilt, his desire to confess and be absolved, and thus with his destruction. Similarly, in *Blind Date*, Jan's youthful idealism gives him, too, strength and honesty. In the crueller world of *King and Country*, Hamp's naïve and inarticulate idealism — his pathetically confused reasons for volunteering, his disbelief that he, a volunteer who has been out at the front since the early days of the war, can be sentenced to death — is not enough to save him from a trap not dissimilar to the one in which van Rooyen found himself caught: the very improbability of the plot of *Blind Date* gives van Rooyen's predicament a kind of nightmarish, Kafkaesque overtone. The presentation which Losey makes here of youthful idealism as naïve and confused takes on added force when one looks back on his career, to the idealism of *The Boy with Green Hair* or *The Lawless*. Losey has commented recently on the sacrifice which Larry Wilder makes in *The Lawless*, to combat the evil of racialism: "I didn't really believe very much in that sacrifice. I think it's a bit sentimental." (P.v.B.). Losey seems to subject not only his own art,

25

but also that of those whom he admires, to this intense critical scrutiny or re-evaluation; for a critic, if, perhaps, not for Losey himself, *King and Country* seems to be a searching re-examination of the attitudes expressed in Kubrick's *Paths of Glory* (a film which he much admires, as he does most of Kubrick's work) as if he felt, perhaps unconsciously, that the character of Colonel Dax is similarly sentimentalised. Certainly in *King and Country* Captain Hargreaves, one of Losey's most complexly Brechtian creations, indulges in that kind of melodramatic overpleading or overstating of the rightness of his case that one had felt to be the basic weakness of Kubrick's film: however, Hargreaves's behaviour is convincingly *placed* within the total framework of the film: whereas Dax (Kirk Douglas) makes indulgently theatrical speeches direct to the audience, speeches which the film seems clearly to endorse, Hargreaves makes similarly theatrical speeches to his fellow officers on the court-martial. The audience is left free to observe and judge the nature of Hargreaves's emotionalism.

One senses that this continual probing and testing of various philosophies and value-systems is not entirely conscious on Losey's part. Rather than being part of a vast intellectual and creative programme, it may simply result from an innate visual sense which Losey himself could perhaps never articulate, that quality, which has been commented on, of knowing exactly what it is that he wants: "The selected reality symbol must be perfect." It may have its root in something as simple as the physical appearance of an actor to whom Losey responds. Appropriately enough, Hardy Kruger (Jan van Rooyen), Stanley Baker (Morgan and Tyvian) and Tom Courtenay (Hamp) are of similar build. Or from a response to some other quality he has sensed in an actor: Stanley Baker has described how he first came to work for Losey; Losey offered him a part which he turned down, "But for some reason or other, reasons only known to himself, I've never really questioned

him on them, he sort of pursued me for the next three years . . .
A few years after I first met him, he asked me to see him again,
and it was about *Blind Date* . . . "(S.B.). Or it may simply derive
from a refusal to accept the easy solution to a creative problem.
When asked about the repetition of certain themes and stories in
his work, Losey replied: "Doesn't every artist in every field more
or less deal with one subject?" then added: "I'm not aware of
such repetitions at all. I really am not conscious of it . . . In fact,
I've tried to . . . , if I find myself doing something that I suddenly
remember I've done before, I try to find another answer."(P.v.B.).

Next in this passage from *Encore* on Brecht, Losey mentions
"The heightening of reality to ennoble"; a couple of pages earlier
he has stated: "Art is larger than life." Losey says of his characters:
"I don't see any of these people either as heroes, or even as anti-
heroes, but simply as prototypes, various kinds of prototypes for
the things that are done to all of us by ourselves and by each other
all the time. This is the essence, for me, of the struggle of understanding life, and of staying alive instead of being dead while
alive, and of making use of life before you're too tired to do anything except wither away." For Losey, the creation of heroes, one
of the traditional literary and theatrical methods of ennobling,
avoids the essential problems: "We've had enough heroes, and
there are few heroes, and this is not the problem. The problem is
how to believe in life, and how to believe in human beings, and
how to believe even in various forms of human existence, re-
cognising that they are archaic, selfish, barbaric, and circumscribed
by an enormous clutter of deceptions." Losey ennobles by building
into the structure of his pictures a poetic rhythm which is not
something purely visual, but rather a rhythmic balance of camera-
movement, soundtrack, acting, and juxtaposition of sequences.
It was this quality in *Eve*, essential to Losey's conception, designed to offset or balance the harshness of the subject matter and

27

the cruelty of some of the treatment, giving one, simultaneously, an intense awareness of both beauty and waste, that the Hakims destroyed by making certain cuts, and mutilating the soundtrack of *Eve*. The poetry of the film, as Losey conceived it, would have implied some kind of way out of, or at least relief from the violence of the central situation — a deliverance through the film's form or aesthetic (C.L.).

"The extension of the vision of the individual *eye*": with this characteristic of Brechtian theatre, an expression of the fundamental challenge of film-making, of artistic creation, Losey concludes his discussion of Brecht and Cinema. "We are all more or less blind," says the young artist Jan van Rooyen, "We can see precisely only those things we work with every day."

2. The Boy with Green Hair

"AT THE time I was about to start *The Boy With Green Hair*, the first hearings began in relation to Hollywood; then *The Boy*, for nearly two years, was a dead issue. All this was happening in and around a period which was steadily getting tougher, and I remember that just about that moment there was a perfectly dreadful, an unbelievably dreadful script that was produced, God knows by whom, called *I Married a Communist*, which was used as a kind of touchstone for whether you were on the right side or not . . .

"The issues are very complex. They're more complex than the film suggests. They're told in pretty over-simplified Hollywood terms. I was working in, knew only, the Hollywood mould and didn't know that very well. I protested, I suppose, within myself, against certain aspects of it, but this is what I used, and this is what I continued to use over here up to and including *Blind Date*, at which point, I think, I left it entirely." *Joseph Losey* (J.D.L.)

"Even in the Middle West, where I was born and brought up, I always felt alien. I *was* very much part of it, but I *was* a foreigner in that I was not part of it in the sense of being willing to belong and be put in a package. And in England, I don't feel at home either. In Italy, I don't feel at home either, but I feel at home everywhere in a sense, so that I am everywhere at home. And it seems to me that one is talking more and more about a world society, and that the sooner the people of the earth begin to feel at home everywhere, and not at home anywhere, the better." *Joseph Losey* (P.v.B.)

The apparent naïvety of form of *The Boy With Green Hair* causes a peculiar tension between the film and the audience: just as Peter looks back to a perhaps somewhat fanciful period of beauty and security when his parents were alive, a period dominated by memories of receiving presents when things were simple, the spectator looks on the fable world which Peter now inhabits with similar nostalgia. The problems of war and peace, of international aid and understanding, are presented in over-simplified child's language. Because one to some extent identifies with Peter, one yearns for a world in which a depiction of the miseries caused by war would be enough to deter nations from going to war. But one shares also Peter's education: one learns that it is not enough to experience a vision of the human suffering caused by war; one must also have the strength and consistency of purpose to make others share that vision, and one can only do that when one has come to terms with the reality of one's own situation and existence, accepted it. Only then can one follow the advice Dr. Evans gives Peter at the end of the film: "Don't get discouraged and run away if you don't succeed at first."

Peter has a very clear picture of the ideal world that ought to be, and a very clear picture of the cruel world of which he has been a victim: there can be no connection between the two worlds until his personality is sufficiently matured for him to create the connections. His vision of the ideal is revealed when Gramp tells him of his love, the acrobat Eileen, who died after a fall from a trapeze. "I didn't think they ever fell," says Peter; "They fall", Gramp replies sadly. We have already seen the other, cruel world in his first conversation with Gramp: sullen, distrusting Gramp's friendliness, Peter takes the initiative: "I think you'd better tell me what rooms I'm allowed to go in." Gramp partially reassures him, but Peter is still distrustful; once Gramp has left the room, Peter takes up a vase and drops it; when Gramp returns to see what has happened, Peter says, questioning yet defiant: "I did it on purpose." Gramp replies simply: "I know what you mean, lad."

Once he has started to establish a secure relationship with Gramp Peter is able to tackle his first problem, his fear of the dark, successfully. "There's nothing in the dark that wasn't there when the light was on," Gramp tells him. Left alone in the dark (Gramp is in show business, and works in the evenings), Peter seems a bit dubious, but he turns the light in his room on again, has a look round, then takes his baseball bat back to bed with him; as he lies in bed, he strokes it, and it seems to give him reassurance. On one level Peter feels, rather naïvely and unrealistically, that it would be a useful weapon to use against an intruder. Then, clearly, the bat is a masculine phallic symbol: the incident is an image of a very tentative dawning acceptance of his male sexuality, an acceptance that can only come with security, but which provides further security. Finally, it is very obviously a symbol of social acceptance: boys at school play baseball, so the bat may be a key to friendship, but, if it goes unused, it is a sign of rejection. Next morning, when we see Peter going to school, we see him through the wire surrounding the playground. The wire is not keeping the children imprisoned within the playground; rather, Peter is trapped outside the community the school forms; the school itself looks friendly enough. The concept of rejection takes us to the core of Peter's personality: he feels that, because his parents left him to go to the war, they did not love him: "They didn't care about me. They just cared about saving other children. They didn't care what happened to me." Thus the two themes stated at the very opening of the movie in the song ("The greatest thing you'll ever learn is just to love and be loved in return"), and by Dr. Evans's comment about "Mr. Nobody . . . has no mother and father", are for Peter intimately connected, and Peter's quest is, in this, a paradigm of the psychoanalytical concept of the maturing individual's quest for identity.

Peter's crisis is provoked by the school's campaign to raise money for war orphans — itself an act of sympathy and compassion. The children on the poster are foreign, sufficiently distant for Peter only partially to recognise his condition in theirs. He tells Dr. Evans: "I knew all along my mother and father were dead. I was just pretending they were on a trip. But I knew." However, he rejects the reality of this knowledge from his consciousness; fascinated by the children on the campaign poster, he asks his teacher: "Are they real children, or are they just made up?" Left alone in the classroom, he tears the poster, which threatens him: he wants not to be an orphan, not to be different, not to have lost his parents, those special objects in whose presence one feels secure. Then, not wishing to harm others worse off than himself, he tries to mend it.

Soon after, he overhears in a store a conversation about war, which triggers off his own fears of death. He goes to bed, thinking of death, his own and his parents', and of spring, and in the morning he wakes up with green hair — a visible sign of his individual condition. At first puzzled, he soon becomes frightened, and turns to Gramp as if he believed in the omnipotence of the one he loves, and who gives him security: "Gramp, please make it go away"; but that is one conjuring trick that even an experienced entertainer like Gramp cannot perform. Gramp's sympathy has caused him to be somewhat over-protective: during the course of the movie he accepts responsibility for his failure in not telling Peter about his parents, thus encouraging Peter to avoid the reality of his situation.

Peter is afraid of having his hair cut off; again, the beautifully clear Freudian overtones of the symbol heighten the complexity of the situation: thus green hair is a symbol of an essential part of the Peter who is, the Peter who must love and win love, the unique Peter whom Peter cannot yet accept: "I want it the way it was." His teacher's well meaning attempts to give him security — "How many boys have brown hair? How many have red hair? . . . and how many have green hair?" are little real help, and they fail to silence the prejudiced: "How'd you like to have your sister marry somebody with green hair?" When the situation becomes unbearable, Peter runs away to the green fields and woods to cry, and there he meets the ghosts, the war orphans from the poster. The sight of them, some crippled, some starving, is a vision which teaches him that the effects of war are far worse than having green hair. Indeed, he learns: "Green is the colour of spring. It means hope"; Peter, who has survived the war, is a symbol of the new life, the new generation that springs out of the destruction of war; his hair is to remind the world "that war is very bad for children." But Peter's conversion to the cause of pacifism, his acceptance of the reasons for his green hair, is too sudden to be anything but superficial, an evasion of his own situation and of those things in himself which he must come to terms with if he is ever to achieve effective and purposeful action. His sudden intense identification with the war orphans is a denial of his own depression: he is crying when

*THE PROWLER: Webb Garwood (Van Heflin), Susan Gilvray
(Evelyn Keyes), and the body of Susan's husband.*

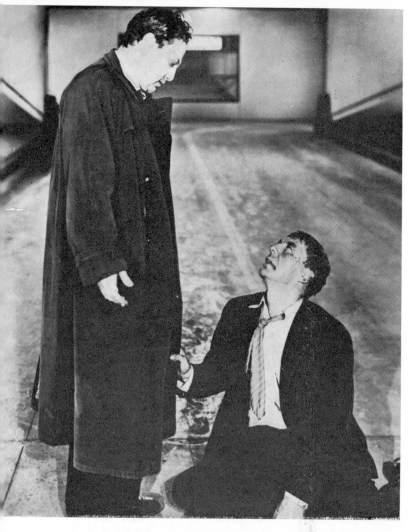

M: "Who killed our children's hopes?"
Langley (Luther Adler) and M (David Wayne).

he meets them, but leaves them fired with his mission. His over-confident expectation of immediate success is one reason why his mission fails. "Nobody believed me. Nobody listened". He experiences another intolerable rejection, and becomes yet again the victim of the hostility of the cruel world he has been in conflict with before. He is chased by his schoolmates, betrayed by another outcast, with whom he might have hoped to establish a sympathy arising from mutual identification, the boy with glasses: "You thought just because I wear glasses I was a sissy". His green hair is shaved off. As it falls from his head Losey shows, in an incredibly beautiful long shot of the barber's shop, all the adults standing around watching falling into an uneasy silence. Only the barber, who was doing his job, is unashamed when it is over. The boy with glasses, whose betrayal was motivated by a desire for acceptance, makes his apology: "Everybody makes fun of me because I wear thick glasses." Peter's fellows have learnt something from the experience, and perhaps are now ready to learn more. But Peter has been shocked into a complete silence which not even Gramp can break: "Peter, you've got to talk to me . . . I'm sorry . . . I feel ashamed." Left alone, Peter runs away, taking his baseball bat and a large handkerchief Gramp had given him.

Picked up by the police, he is brought face to face with Dr. Evans; it is the interview which ensues that opens the movie: like *Blind Date*, *Eve*, and a minor film *The Intimate Stranger*, *The Boy With Green Hair* is told largely in flashback. Each of these three movies is centrally concerned with at least one character's relationship to his past, or vision of his past. For Peter, as for Jan in *Blind Date*, the experience of relating his story (or his version of his story — we see the action through Peter's eyes, and Dr. Evans comments: "I'm not really concerned with whether the boy's hair was green or not. I believe in what he says, that's what matters.") is an act of therapy which enables him to accept the reality of his situation, and come to terms with his past. Dr. Evans's friendly acceptance of Peter as an ordinary boy, and as an equal, makes this therapeutic experience possible, and defines our attitude to Gramp's over-protectiveness. Once he has relived his past traumas, Peter is able to accept Gramp's love again, and through Gramp his parents' love, a love which once truly existed but is now lost forever. Gramp reads Peter his father's letter of love and explanation, a letter which turns a poignant memory into a past reality which can be a source of strength. "We had a job to do," Peter's father writes: "It was because of our great love for you"; of death he writes: "It need not be sad if the gift has been well used"; and he gives Peter a task: "If they forget, remind them." Now he has come to terms with his past, found love and security, and accepted his identity, Peter is no longer the boy with green hair; he is in a position to accept the gift of life and use it well: to remind those who forget.

Some people may object that the terms used in this discussion ("rejection", "quest for identity", "denial of depression") turn a simple childlike fable into something forbiddingly intellectual, but the film's naïvely pure vision has too often caused it to be dismissed by modern sophisticates as a sentimental tear-jerker, something which it very clearly is not.

3. The Lawless

"*THE Lawless, The Prowler*, and *M* were all made in a very short period of time, working very rapidly and very intensely. I think they benefited from this, and I think I also benefited enormously in terms of a rather quick development, which came out of a couple of years of work uninterrupted by promotions, which take up so much of one's time now . . . Certainly *The Lawless*

belongs to a very early period of thinking for me . . . I was still trying
to get out of my system, I suppose, some things which were very
much a part of me in the thirties and the early forties . . . My
period of the thirties extended beyond the thirties for all kinds of
reasons — slowness in realising changes after the death of Roosevelt, delay in coming to Hollywood . . . But I think it took a long
time for many of us to get rid of the thirties, and it took a long
time, too, for me to get rid of being overawed by Hollywood, and
by its self-assurance and apparent authority, and this resulted, to
some extent, in fighting harder, perhaps, than one had to, and I
think the pictures suffered, to some extent, from that, and certainly
one's self suffered emotionally a great deal of wear and tear . . .
The music got out of my hands, and it has a banal and horrible
score that I fought as much as I could. The cutting I was able
to control to some extent. I would have wished to eliminate a good
deal of the melodrama from the script, particularly in relation to
the supposed rape of the girl. The thing that interested me, of
course, was the relationship between the white and Mexican
community, and also the question of responsibility, the Macdonald
Carey part, the newspaper owner-proprietor . . .

"There's no doubt that the American social structure is very
simple, and often, therefore, very contradictory: sometimes very
benign, sometimes very malignant, sometimes very tolerant, sometimes a lynch mob." *Joseph Losey* (J.D.L.)

The Lawless is about fear, man's struggle to master fear, his
successes and failures. For the young white Americans the fear
is connected with a general teenage sexual insecurity: they set
out to prove their masculinity by forcing their attentions on the
Mexican girls. (When one sees the bitchy white girl the reporter
Jonas Creel is dating, one tends to understand this insecurity. In
Jonas, too, we detect a fear, the fear of failure; a sense that being

a small-town reporter is not enough.) For the members of the "lynch mob", the fear is similar; violence becomes a symbol of masculinity: "Looks like some of us have forgotten how to be men". For Paul Rodriguez, the fear is, essentially, fear of the trap that is closing in about him — a trap that is symbolic of the society in which he lives. Though Paul has American citizenship, though his brother died on the Normandy beachhead, to most of the white Americans with whom he comes into contact, he and his friends will always be Mexicans — "lazy good-for-nothings", in the words of his employer. He tries to live up to the ideal that his brother represents to him, but a moment of panic when he slugs a cop in a brawl at a dance precipitates him on to a desperate, pathetic, illogical rush to escape, to run away from the problems that living in such a community as that of Santa Marta, the self-styled "friendly city", necessarily involves. Paul's flight is the central image of the movie, relating as it does to the attempts of the central character, Larry Wilder the newspaper proprietor, to run away from *his* problems, and it drags Paul deeper and deeper into an ever worsening situation, till, when he is cornered, he is found crying like a child. As Larry Wilder says in his editorial, Paul's only crime was fear.

Larry himself is afraid of losing his paper, and with it his chance of obtaining the things that he really wants from life. Although he has won fame as a crusading reporter, he has always retained his dream-like memories of childhood in a small town: "I had all that once. And I want it again," he tells the Mexican girl, Sunny, trying to explain his dream. Sunny has followed his career; she has gotten inspiration from him, just as Paul Rodriguez gets it from his dead brother.

After the brawl, which was precipitated by white troublemakers, Larry refused to support the Mexicans. He had been at the dance, but did not see, having escaped into a waltz with Sunny, or chose not to have seen, how the trouble started. "You know what upset me most back there?" Sunny asks, "You. Running away from a fight. Do you know what it meant when you said you weren't taking sides any more?" Just as Paul is cornered by the hostile members of the society from which he is fleeing, Larry is cornered by his need for self-respect, and, perhaps, by his own loneliness. He has his paper, true, but his attitude as soon as he meets Sunny makes it clear that he wants something more: sex, understanding, sympathy, love, all four, perhaps. After their first evening together, he wants to kiss her goodnight. "It was to have been a very respectful kiss," he says; "I don't doubt it," she replies; "I do," he says, "I keep my respectful kisses for my mother." "So do I," she replies. From the very first, he is making a pass at her, and one cannot help but feel that a beautiful wife may well be an integral part of his small-town dream. He becomes involved in Paul's story as much out of a need for Sunny's affection and respect as out of any idealism, and he, too, gets dragged in deeper and deeper, until, like the essentially harmless and completely helpless Paul, he is shot at by the mob of Paul's pursuers. He learns what it is to be hunted like a Mexican boy from the wrong side of the tracks, a victim of prejudice and bad luck; he therefore comes to understand what it is to have only Sleepy Hollow, the Mexican quarter, to run to. But if, during the course of the film, Larry learns, or re-learns, the lesson of compassion for the oppressed, Sunny learns understanding and sympathy for Larry and his conflict. When they first met, she begged him to use his paper to "Tell the people across there to look across the track"; "You're looking at a tired man", he replied. Later, she hopes that Larry will use his paper to tell the truth about Paul, but now she realises: "For the first time in your life, you've got what you want." "Thanks. For understanding", Larry replies. Though his developing relationship with Sunny (she has already kissed him as thanks for arranging with the Chief of Police for Paul's parents to see their son. She says it's Paul's mother thanking him. Larry replies: "She has sweet lips.") is a major force in making him decide to publish an editorial pleading for Paul, there are certainly other factors at work — the irresponsibility of Jan Dawson's reporting: "Rodriguez stood there. Mud-covered. Sullen . . ."; the attempt by some of the town's businessmen to pressure him into silence.

Larry's relationship with Sunny, Larry's final decision, are all part of a total social context which Losey creates with his usual vivid awareness of the complexity of truth. (One wonders what he might have done with *High Noon*, a project with which his name was once associated; he might conceivably have made the Gary Cooper/Grace Kelly relationship emotionally convincing!). Jonas Creel, for example, is rather pathetic in his desire to get on; yet it is this desire that first draws in the newspapermen from outside. Paul does, indeed, look mud-covered and sullen after his arrest. Jan Dawson may well be sympathetic to Mrs. Rodriguez, and only acts as she does because she knows the kind of story her paper expects from her; on the other hand, it may be that she consoles Mrs. Rodriguez only because she may need to get a story from her later on. In the original car crash that first sparked off the conflict between the young Mexicans and the young whites, the Mexicans were guilty of careless driving, and the cop who handles the situation is fair and decent. There is even a kind of accuracy in the remark about Larry's editorial made by Mildred's father when he sees Sunny come out of Larry's office (Mildred is the girl Paul is supposed to have assaulted): "It ain't hard to see why you said it"; Sunny has, in fact, just embraced Larry passionately in thanks for the stand he has taken; when he asks her, she tells him that this time it is *she* who was thanking him.

Losey has said that Fritz Lang's *Fury* was an influence in the making of this film, but whereas in *Fury* Spencer Tracy was the victim of a purely malevolent series of coincidences, the pieces of bad luck that ensnare Paul are intimately connected with the tensions and prejudices of the Santa Marta community. In Lang's film, the mass media, coming in from outside, broke the conspiracy of silence plotted by the small town's leading and "responsible businessmen", and demonstrated the guilt of the community. For Losey, the mass media are deeply guilty and responsible, pandering to the worst prejudices and desire for sensationalism of their public; his equivalent of Lang's lynch mob marches not to hang a suspected kidnapper, but to destroy Larry's paper for not telling them what they wanted to hear. And already the police are pandering to the mass media, taking their representatives on a man hunt. "Can we have him right here, in front of the camera, chief?" says a TV reporter; Paul's arrest takes on the quality of a public spectacle. In this society, the responsible businessmen, particularly Joe Ferguson, Senior, are the community's major force for progress: "Maybe we should get rid of Sleepy Hollow. It shouldn't have been there in the first place," Ferguson says. At the end of the film, Ferguson's arguments help to persuade Larry to stay on in Santa Marta: "A lot of people will hate to see you leave . . . Somebody's going to put out a newspaper here." Larry's responsibilities as a newspaperman do not end with the running of one outspokenly provocative editorial. A healthy community would not permit conditions such as those in Sleepy Hollow, and would tolerate an honest newspaper, just as an honest newspaper could help build a healthy community. Ferguson learns, like Larry, that his vision of a small town community is somewhat idealised: "I don't like what happened today. I didn't think it could happen here." At the start, he was the embodiment of liberal paternalistic charity, paying the fines of the nine Mexicans arrested in the brawl, as well as that of his son, the only white boy to be arrested. Larry remarks tolerantly "Maybe he has a guilty conscience about his son." Sunny

39

replies bitterly, though perhaps accurately: "So he eases his conscience, gets us to admit we're wrong." Ferguson does believe that his money can charm conflicts away, and he is wrong. His son Joe is as prejudiced as any of his fellow teenage troublemakers, and he bitterly resents his father's refusal to back him up: one senses a history of some kind of failure in this relationship that goes beyond the particular issue of anti-Mexican feeling. Eventually, young Joe Ferguson learns not from his father's example, but from a possibly general feeling of remorse that the townspeople experience after the destruction of Larry's newspaper. One senses that the character of Joe Ferguson, Senior, represents some kind of expression of Losey's (perhaps critical) sympathy with the attitudes and achievements of the Roosevelt era, which ended shortly before the film was made; if so, one could argue that the destructive attitudes lurking below the surface are not dissimilar to those unleashed shortly afterwards in the days of McCarthy. Losey's Larry Wilder stays on in Santa Marta to attempt to bring out a newspaper on the old and inadequate presses of the Spanish language weekly that Sunny works for. *The Lawless* was made in 1949; in 1951, when Losey's name came up before the Congressional Investigating Committee, Losey was not given the same freedom of choice.

4. The Prowler

"I THINK that to a certain extent it did come off. I liked the actors, and we got on well together. I had more rehearsal on that than on any other picture before or since. Van Heflin was essentially theatre trained. I'd known him before. I was using Evelyn Keyes, an actress not very much seen. I had great co-operation from the writers — of whom there were several — and also from Spiegel, and I was given the most expert, willing, interested and professional technical crew. It had, again, to be shot very fast, and it was shot very fast. I saw it again this year, and I must say I was very disappointed in it. I think I was primarily disappointed because it seems to me now, as much as, maybe more than *The Lawless*, to be a period piece, a piece that really belongs, in a sense, to the thirties or early forties, and I don't recognise myself in relation to that. It's not quite far enough away for me to accept it as a period piece. There are certain techniques developing that I recognise, and done very well, I think, like the many sustained shots, but basically the script attitudes and my attitudes were a bit primitive and a bit Hollywood and a bit over-dialogued . . . It was a complete picture because I knew exactly what I wanted, and everybody working on it liked everybody else. They liked the picture — the crew liked it, Evelyn Keyes liked it, and was marvellous to work with. All the lesser actors liked it, we liked the locations, even Spiegel liked it."

"I think the girl is a very complex character."

"Yes, she's also a product of the thing that happens so often in America, and still happens everywhere that I know of in the West. In spite of all the pretensions which have grown up and have to some extent been realised, the wife is left alone, presumably with everything to see she's comfortable, but with no friends, with no values excepting those from her childhood, with no love, essentially, and in this case with no children." *Joseph Losey* (J.D.L.)

The Prowler, like *The Servant*, is a perfect film. Like *The Servant*, it gives a full and valid picture of a certain kind of society and attitude toward life; every gesture, every incident, is intended to make a point, and does so. Like *The Servant*, it is a masterpiece of craftsmanship, a technical *tour de force* in which everything Losey attempts comes off — the use of sets or soundtrack to heighten a

41

situation, to express the tension or conflict or guilt underlying a situation (an example of this, not the most subtle, is the sudden memory of the dead Gilvray that is evoked by the sound of his voice coming from a tape which has somehow got in among those Susan and Webb have taken with them to the ghost town in the Mojave Desert). Yet, like *The Servant*, it seems to lack something that some of Losey's other, less perfect, less complete movies (say *M* from his early period; *The Damned* or the mutilated *Eve* from more recent years) have contained — passion, emotion, some kind of intensity — and without this, despite its very considerable virtues, the film remains to some extent an intellectual exercise, a work of art which one can respect, but one which affects one less deeply. Losey's direction seems to be as coldly calculating as Webb Garwood's manipulation of those who he uses or exploits during the course of the film. It is true that, at certain moments, we feel sympathy for Garwood as someone pathetically wrong, a victim (of false values) as much as an exploiter, yet even those moments seem to be calculated rather than deeply felt. Losey feels compassion for Garwood, as he does for Barrett in *The Servant*, as a victim of a system he does not fully understand. He reveals both Garwood and Barrett as vulnerable, but he somehow fails to make us share the compassion that such a revelation implies that he feels for them. This is particularly true of his handling of Garwood: when he has finally got what he wants — Susan, the motel — he displays no true emotional response to his situation, coolly eyeing a pretty girl who is booking into his motel for the night. Webb is just too nasty to hold our compassion; the character of Barrett is very much more successful in this respect. This is partly because *The Servant* is an extremely witty film; also because, though Barrett uses Vera, they do have some fun together: for example, one responds very strongly to both of them when they sample the luxury of Tony's bathroom. Thus one feels Barrett's vulnerability more intensely than Garwood's.

42

In both *The Prowler* and *The Servant*, one detects an absence of intense feeling, not just in the characters, but in the director, which seems to be intimately linked with an excess of intellectual calculation and directorial control, and with the perfection or completeness of the movies. It is as if Webb Garwood and Hugo Barrett were profoundly and intimately linked with, even symbolic of, one strand — not, perhaps the most creative — of Losey's artistic personality. The theme of coldly calculated manipulation seems to fascinate Losey so much in these films, particularly in *The Prowler*, that one aspect of his normally very rich and complex *mise-en-scène* — a strain of coldly calculating intellectuality — becomes dominant at the expense of the others — his passion, his sense of cinematic rhythm and poetry — and to the detriment of the film.

"Didn't you have enough pull?" asks Webb Garwood, questioning Susan Gilvray about the failure of her career on the stage; "I was just a little short of talent," she replies. For Garwood, success as a human being is intimately connected with the size and ornateness of one's house (he is very impressed by Gilvray's house), with the amount of money one earns, and it comes not through genuine ability or achievement, but through "pull"; failure is purely a question of "bad breaks." Garwood's commitment to a vision of the world as a place of ruthless competition is sufficiently one-sided or warped to be mildly pathological, yet it is intimately connected with many of the underlying assumptions of the world in which he lives. "I'm not any worse than anybody else," he claims, and he does stand for a very real force in contemporary society, and one which may, at times, overwhelm or deceive other, more constructive forces in society. Garwood's fellow patrolman, Bud Crocker — a personification of duty and loyalty — is exultant when the inquest exonerates Garwood from any blame in Gilvray's death. One senses, indeed, that a man less trusting than Crocker, one less likely to be taken in by Garwood, might also be one who

43

was less likely to find in routine police work and mundane hobbies as satisfying an existence as Crocker does: there are times when Crocker bores the audience almost as much as he does Webb. If Garwood is symbolic of a certain kind of competitive materialism, his story is symbolic of the fact that such a credo is ultimately self-defeating and destructive. Garwood has once already glimpsed success and affluence, and tasted failure: a brilliant basketballer (Susan remembers his skill from high school days) he won a sports scholarship to a university, which he ultimately lost because his coach said he couldn't play with a team. His chance meeting with Susan sparks off a series of confused emotions and attitudes. She is a rich man's beautiful possession, and thus fair game for one who covets money and possessions. Yet there are moments of possibly genuine affection: they share memories when they discover that they both come from the same town; they are both lonely. Gilvray, Susan's husband, is much older than her; he broadcasts on a late-night show, leaving Susan alone in the house. The marriage seems to be a loveless failure; there are no children, and Gilvray's habit of recording all his radio programmes (there is a great cabinet of them in the house) indicates some kind of egotistic obsession. Webb is able to offer Susan a physical sexuality that is lacking in her marriage. However, once Webb has gained control over Susan, he is callously sadistic in his treatment of her, trying to make her do what he wants, turn her into his possession; he has no sympathy for the difficulties she has when her husband starts to suspect she has a lover. His dominating obsession — money — counterbalances any emotional attachment he has had to Susan; she becomes a pawn in the game he is to play with society in his quest for affluence: if Gilvray dies, Susan will be rich, so Webb kills Gilvray during a patrol (shooting himself, too, to make the "accident" convincing — a beautifully concise image of the detailed calculation of which Garwood is capable). Susan guesses the truth, but Webb's skill in handling people (the dead man's brother, then Susan herself) brings him success: he gets his girl, her husband's money, and buys the motel of which he had dreamed: a motel makes money for you even while you sleep!

On their first night together at the motel Susan reveals that she is expecting Webb's baby, a baby conceived during their affair before her husband's death, and some months before their marriage: Webb has left the most simple and obvious of the forces of life out of his calculations.

The baby immediately becomes, for Webb, a symbol of his guilt: it cannot be born in a hospital, as then questions would be asked, and Webb knows that Gilvray's brother, and possibly others, are aware of the fact that Gilvray was infertile. The pathological reaction that the news about the baby provokes in Webb — fear, anger and rejection rather than love and warmth — is comment enough on the nature of the values and dreams which motivate him. Webb's callousness towards Susan makes one feel that Susan's marriage to Gilvray had left her so desperate that she was incapable of seeing and responding to Webb as he is. It is as if, wanting a baby, rather than Webb's baby in particular, she has unconsciously used him in much the way that he has used her. Like Webb, Susan is only partly able to achieve communication with others, being limited by her own obsessions. Though these are clearly not destructive in the way that Webb's are, they are still obsessions. The baby may symbolise a creative life force, but an essential part of a genuinely creative life force is the ability of human beings to respond to each other: one senses Susan needs the baby too much to be a genuinely good mother.

Susan does, however, succeed in melting Webb — again it is difficult to know exactly what emotions are being expressed in their relationship, but one senses the kind of bond that comes when human beings turn to each other for comfort, something which is not love, but might conceivably grow into love — and they agree that she shall have her baby in secret. Thus, Webb's quest for money, and for the possessions and place in society that come with it, culminates in a flight away from society and from his possessions to a small ghost town in the Mojave Desert[3], where Susan can have her baby without there being anyone around to recognise them, and ask awkward questions.

Once again, though, life is something that cannot be controlled by the calculations of the human intellect. Susan's delivery is difficult, and Webb's policeman's knowledge of childbirth cannot handle it, so Webb, desperate at Susan's plight, is forced to fetch a doctor, who is easily able to deliver the child. Susan has discovered that Webb has deceived her (she finds his gun, which Webb said he sold after the "accidental" shooting of her husband as he felt he could never handle a gun again) and fearing that Webb may kill again — the doctor may have recognised them — she warns the doctor, and helps him to escape by hiding Webb's car keys. Webb is shot down attempting to flee from the trap his actions have built around him — destroyed by the unpredictability of life and the emotions, which no calculation, however careful, can control; by the conflict between his grasping individualism and his confused commitment to another person, Susan; by his own false values, which are a denial of life. Life cannot be denied.

---

[3] The Mojave Desert has an iconographical significance all its own; like *The Prowler*, Erich von Stroheim's *Greed* ends there; just as Brecht's *City of Mahagony* was built in the middle of a desert by a group of gangsters on the run from the city, so the pleasure centre of Las Vegas was founded on what was probably syndicate money in the middle of the Mojave.

5. M

"I HAD no battles with Spiegel on *The Prowler* at all — that was fortunately one happy experience early on. Nor did I have any battles with the producer of *The Boy with Green Hair*, but only with the management. Nor did I have any trouble on *M*, excepting that I was bound to the structure of the original picture and script because this was a condition made when the film was passed by — I don't know whether it was then the Breen Office, or still the Hays Office, but they said they would pass *M* provided it was a remake of what they considered to be a classic, so there had to be a certain adherence to the structure of the original, although the intent and the point of my film was entirely different. I'd seen *M* in the early thirties; I saw it again, once, in a very bad copy, just before I made it. I never referred to it. I only consciously repeated one shot. There may have been unconscious repetitions, in terms of the atmosphere of certain sequences, but essentially Lang's villain was my hero.

"It's a picture, of course, that's been terribly mutilated in Europe. And, I'm informed, it was banned in many states in the U.S.A. Many of these pictures that have suffered from censorship could now be re-shown, of course. I regarded it then as a far better picture than *The Lawless*, even though it was an uneven picture, partly because it was more ambitious, more complex, and it was more developed from my point of view."

"The underworld worked in Lang . . ."

"It didn't work here. The underworld of Lang, the underworld written in the text which we had to follow basically, made no sense in terms of Los Angeles in the 1940's or early fifties, and I tried to get over this a bit by using a good deal of old Los Angeles. Bits of it are very modern, bits are very old: the old Victorian houses that were on a ridge overlooking the dividing line between the city of

Los Angeles and Hollywood, which was developing very rapidly beyond. I believe that part of Los Angeles is now entirely gone." — *Joseph Losey* (J.D.L.)

"I think that some of the best work I've ever done is in *M*. It's again a very uneven film, and it suffered from the fact that I had to stick to the structure of the original, because of censorship. But there were two or three very long scenes that I think — I thought at the time, I haven't seen it for eight or ten years — which I think were exceptionally played and shot, and I don't know, the British censors cut, oh, two-thirds of these scenes, right out of the middle of the takes, because they were all one shot." — *Joseph Losey* (P.v.B.)

If Garwood is at one pole, coldly manipulating his fellow creatures into trusting and respecting him, the child-murderer in *M* is at the other, driven by an insane, perverted passion over which he has no control, provoking the hatred and distrust of his fellows, giving them a chance to express their own irrational and destructive impulses by attempting to lynch him. These same perverted emotions that make M an object for hatred and fear make him also somehow more human, more sympathetic, less evil than Garwood, who much of the time seems emotionally dead. A similar opposition occurs in a later film, *The Criminal*, where one is left wondering who is the more sinister, the more evil, the deeply emotional sadist Barrows, or the emotionally dead Mike Carter.

Garwood, too, is very much a product of his society, accepting and embodying many of its most potent non-values and assumptions; an extreme product, perhaps, but not untypical. M is essentially in reaction against his society, and against himself as a product of that society. His reaction is so intense it leads him to reject the concept of human life altogether: "My mother said men are born evil and cruel." With his flute, he's like a kind of Pied Piper, pro-

*THE BIG NIGHT: George La Main (John Barrymore Jnr.)
and Marion Rostina (Joan Lorring). Losey handles
their tentative advances and recoils with beautiful delicacy.*

THE SLEEPING TIGER: Frank Clements (Dirk Bogarde), Glenda Esmond (Alexis Smith), and Sally (Patricia McCarron). Displacement: Frank's revenge on Glenda and on his step-mother could at first only be taken on Sally.

THE INTIMATE STRANGER: a production meeting, with Reggie Wilson (Richard Basehart), and Ernie Chapple (Mervyn Johns). It is not that these men irresponsibly exploit their audience, just that they have nothing to say.

tecting children by taking them out of the evil society into which they are born, a world that is too cruel for children. "What is there to look forward to unless the children grow up better than us?" he asks, when dragged before the kangaroo court of the underground. The "court" is a typical product of the society M rejects, a product of a compulsive revengeful hysteria that is quite out of control. M's condition is intimately connected with the false values that his society worships: the hospitals are under-staffed, which is one reason why he is free. Because they are understaffed, he may be executed when he is arrested; even a real court of law exacts from the guilty the revenge which society demands. "He'll burn," says a detective gleefully; "That's right. That's right," says Carney, his superior, bitterly, "That'll fix everything". By finding and punishing a scapegoat, society will once again avoid facing up to its responsibilities and attempting to tackle its fundamental problems. Throughout the movie, society is presented as being brutal and irrational — witness the incidents that occur when the public is alerted to protect children from the killer: several embryo lynch-mobs spring up, aggressive and cruel to their suspect rather than protective to the child they think may be in danger. There is little real difference in behaviour between ordinary citizens and the members of the underworld, who turn their search for M (he has hidden in a block of offices and businesses just before it is locked up at the end of the working day) into an orgy of destruction, smashing glass, breaking in doors.

There are many nice touches in Losey's handling of the under-world. Where Lang's underworld bosses use a Peachum-like army of beggars (shades of *The Threepenny Opera*!), Losey's use the apparently legitimate fleet of taxis that they own. A member of a gang cannot leave his territory, even in pursuit of the child-murderer: the detail of the underworld has been closely enough observed, but what is lacking (as a result of the pressures exerted on Losey by his having to conform to the plot of the original) is any sense of its place in the total social structure of the community. One did not sense this lack in Lang's *M*, probably because, in the stylised society he was presenting, there was not the interpenetration between the underworld and respectable society that is symbolised by the underworld's "Ajax" taxi-fleet. (Lang himself was able to handle this aspect of American society more convincingly in an entirely new film, *The Big Heat*.) And precisely because Lang's underworld was so completely separate a community, one is more willing to accept that the manhunt for the child-killer is a real threat to it, and thus the motivations of the underworld leaders become, in the context established by the film, more acceptable than they are in the Losey. In the Los Angeles context, the underworld leader's desire to win the public's sympathy by catching "the baby-killer" somehow rings false.

In this cruel society, only two men show any kind of rationality — Carney and the underworld boss — and only two show any humanity — Carney and Langley, the drunken lawyer who defends M before the underworld court. Langley is a potentially rational man, but has been destroyed by a compulsion as uncontrollable as M's — his drinking, which seems to be, at least in part, an expression of guilt for his activities on behalf of the underworld. The sadistic treatment he has received from the boss of the underworld gives him genuine compassion for M; he has been ordered by his boss to defend M, as a lynching would not fit in with the plan to win public sympathy, but he responds to the strange, pathetic truth of M's picture of life and society, and rounds on his boss. "Who killed our children's hopes?" Those like the leaders of the underworld, and others, who have a vested interest in society as it is, who combat the changes that will enable the children to grow up better than us, are the ones who are truly guilty. Langley's accusation results in his being shot down by his boss, and Carney arrives in time to arrest two murderers. M says of Langley: "He was a good man; he's been punished. Now it's my turn."

M differs from society in that he recognises his guilt; he is pathological because the burden of that guilt is crippling; he has been warped by punishments inflicted on him when he was a child, by his memories of his father, whom he attacks in his desperate speech to the "court", of his mother, whom he says suffered. He is frustrated in a hostile, alien society which does not understand beauty or gentleness: one of the most complex scenes in the movie comes when M is masturbating to a piece of classical music coming over the radio, sadistically twisting a shoe-lace (from the shoe of one of his victims). The music stops unexpectedly; the half-hour programme is over, and the radio starts to pour out its usual fare of commercials and jingles. M turns it off, and searches desperately for a clay model, resembling both a phallus and a human figure, which he finds near a photo of his mother. He "strangles" the figure, reaching his climax as the "head" falls off: the action is an expression of sexuality, and simultaneously of self-castration, of destruction and self-destruction. M's flute, similarly, is an image of male sexuality, something with which he can create beauty; something which he uses to charm children before he kills them; something which he destroys in his desperate attempt to escape from the trap into which he runs, the room in the office-block.

No one single factor is responsible for making M what he is, and what he is is not exactly clear: the masturbation scene is an expression of intense sado-masochism, but M's murders are motivated by compassion for his victims, whom he does not rape, or abuse sexually in any way. Deeply marked by his social experience, he murders to save children from the sadistic cruelty which he knows to exist in society precisely because he knows it to exist in himself.

51

If, then, society's cruelty, immaturity and rejection of its guilt can first help produce an M, then conveniently turn him into a scapegoat, progress can only come from the efforts of those who, like Carney, can stand outside it, rejecting its assumptions with a combination of self-control, compassion and intellect. Repeatedly in the film, the public acts with childish or hysterical irrationality. M himself is a helpless, guilty child, capable, when under tension, of crying over such a simple thing as spilling a glass of whiskey. It is his own helplessness that makes him identify with such pathological intensity with the helplessness of children. The whiskey incident is placed very close to a moment when Carney, hurriedly tying his shoes, breaks his lace: the broken shoe lace (in the context of M's obsession with shoes, and the use to which he puts shoe-laces) does far more than merely draw attention to a clue which pushes the plot along. It provides a concise, if simple, definition of a mature, unhysterical attitude to external reality as something that can be annoying, but which exists, and which one must come to terms with, calmly — and use, creatively.

6. The Big Night

"THE LAST film I made in Hollywood, *The Big Night*, was completely re-cut, and stupidly re-cut." *Joseph Losey* (P.v.B.)
" 'We're all lonely . . . We've got to have somebody who knows what bothers us.' It's this sort of line which, I think, gives the picture its peculiar Gothic American flavour. Here, union by desperation is taken for granted." *T. J. Ross* (F.C.)

M is about a man so crippled by his own and society's cruelty and guilt that he remains always a helpless child. *The Big Night* is about a child who, in one night, encounters for the first time, and learns to accept, society's guilt, and his own complicity in it, who, therefore, takes a decisive step towards general emotional maturity and freedom.

When we first see George La Main, he is timid, bespectacled, persecuted, a victim of his tough fellow adolescents (one recalls the conflict the younger bespectacled boy in *The Boy with Green Hair* had over gaining acceptance into the group). It is his birthday, and his tough bartender father (his mother is presumably dead) presents him, in the bar, with a cake covered with seventeen lighted candles: an image of the womb-like security and comfort of the family circle. The party atmosphere is destroyed by the irruption into the bar of the sadistic, crippled sports reporter Al Judge, and two of his henchmen. At a command from Judge, Andy La Main strips to the waist to receive a whipping of brutal intensity from Judge's cane — a whipping that seems as if it will never end. George has to be held back, to restrain him from going to his father's defence; the reason for the whipping is kept secret from him; it is something he can't be expected and shouldn't try to understand. Yet it is something he must understand if he is to come to terms with himself and his society.

George sets off with a gun, into the night and the streets, to obtain revenge on his father's assailant, whose identity he does not at first know, plunging deep into the nightmare world of violent, loveless, guilt-ridden relationships. He pursues Judge first to a boxing-match (a neat image of society's love of vicarious violence), where he is robbed by Peckinpaugh, a thug posing as a cop (the implications are obvious). Then an apparently helpful and friendly older man, Lloyd Cooper, takes him under his wing, introducing him to a night-club, and to his mistress, Julie Rostina. At first George is impressed by Cooper, by his knowledge of the world, by the image of sexual success he represents. Yet one wonders why Cooper asked the boy along, unless he felt the need of admiration, or is afraid of an evening alone with Julie, or both. Later it is revealed that Cooper is a professor, and has a wife and children living out of town; Julie has turned to him, not for money, but out of loneliness. She is trapped by her needs in a relationship with a mean, selfish and sometimes violent man: at one point during a quarrel, Cooper violently pushes her down on a chair. T. J. Ross has pointed out *(op. cit.)* that the scene looks forward to the restaurant scene in *The Servant*, where several couples are shown trapped in mutually exploitive relationships, a bleak image of "loveless love." It also looks back to the attitudes towards sex of the white teenagers in *The Lawless*. George's attention is distracted from the cruel relationship of his companions by the club's coloured singer, who represents an image of beauty to him. When he leaves the club, he sees her coming out, with her pet dog on a lead. He tells her how much he enjoyed her singing, and she is touched, smiling kindly back at him. Then the need to communicate forces him into uttering the cruellest of remarks: "I think you are beautiful, even though you are . . . " He does not intend to be cruel; society has so conditioned his attitudes that his unthinking remarks can be deeply hurting. The singer hurries away from him, into the night. He calls after her: "I didn't mean it."

George accompanies Julie and Cooper back to the flat which Julie shares with her younger sister, Marion. As soon as Cooper learns that his association with George may involve him in a scandal that might reach the papers (George has not given up his quest for revenge on Al Judge, and he has already exacted some revenge on Peckinpaugh, who tried to intimidate him a second time) Cooper wants nothing more to do with him, but the girls take him in.

Marion is blonde, simultaneously simple (in her experience) and knowing (as a result of her nearness to Julie and Cooper's relationship), anxious to communicate with George, to help him. Losey handles their tentative advances and recoils with beautiful delicacy: they want to trust each other, but dare not. Perhaps on a less nightmarishly "big" night they could achieve confidence and understanding, though the all-pervasive strain of bitterness and cruelty is there, too: Marion, wanting to help George, to prevent him from doing something he might regret, hides the gun, and George rounds on her savagely.

In the morning, George starts on his odyssey again; he finally corners Al Judge, and is cornered in turn by society and its guilt-laden relationships. He learns that Al Judge's sister had been his father's mistress; that she had killed herself when his father had decided to end the relationship. He learns, too, that his mother is not dead. She drank, and took lovers, and eventually left his father, who then took up with Judge's sister. The parallel between, say, Andy La Main and Lloyd Cooper is all the more affecting and profound precisely because it is nowhere stressed: it exists only when the spectator is alert enough to make it, though it exists too, perhaps unconsciously, in the mind of George.

George shoots Al Judge in a scuffle, refusing, as he did in the second incident with Peckinpaugh, to go on being a victim. When he returns home, he finds his father knows about the shooting, and is preparing to take the blame on himself, to cover up, and hide the truth once again. George refuses to let him do this. He has learnt that the only way to come to terms with guilt is to face up to it, and accept it, to reject the secret conspiracy of guilt, and the crippling burden it involves.

7. Stranger on the Prowl

" *I CAN'T really ask you about* Stranger on the Prowl *because I haven't ever been able to see it.*"

"I again hated the music on it. I disagreed with it entirely. And

55

when the film was delivered to United Artists, they cut a great deal out of it, and changed the title, having removed my credit, and I never saw it in that version at all. I believe it's been shown on the air in the United States, and I heard recently that it had been re-shown in Rome as Joseph Losey's *Stranger on the Prowl*, which is a bit crazy. It started as really quite an interesting script, but still in the Hollywood mould, but it violates a convention about which I have come to be almost fanatic. I think that it's possible in the theatre to have a lot of English or American actors or for that matter, Italians, let's say, speaking in their own language and pretending to be, let's say Germans, or, vice versa, Germans speaking German pretending to be Americans. I don't think it's possible in the cinema. I can't tell you precisely why. It has something to do, I think, with what people so often describe as the realistic aspects of film. They say: 'It's a realistic medium'. The two big clichés are 'It's a realistic medium' and 'It's a story-telling medium'. I think it *is* realistic; I think it *is* story-telling, but I don't think they should be limiting. Well, that picture certainly violated my feeling about language, which has developed to the point where I simply will not shoot a picture unless I can find a way around this problem, unless I can make the language being spoken at any given time credible. This is one of the things I tried to do, *did* do with *Eve*, and one of the most important things that was ruined by the general wrecking of the sound. There, when people spoke English, if they were Italians they spoke with an Italian accent, if French, with a French accent, and they spoke English only when they were talking to someone who didn't speak their language. And in the few places where it was essential for Italians to speak Italian to each other, or French people to speak French to each other, they did, and without subtitles, of course. Apart from language there are various accents. One gets into endless trouble, of course, in dubbing. Stanley Baker's character was based on his Welsh

56

background in *Eve* as it was in the case of *Blind Date*, and this cannot be translated into any other language. I don't know how you would convey the bible-background, the coal-mining background, the particular quality of the accent, the class implications of the accent, even the minorities thing that comes into the whole Welsh idiom. Then you get something like *King and Country* where you have an officer speaking with an upper-class accent, and Tom Courtenay speaking with a very Cockney accent, where this is an essential thing, and where there are various gradations of class and breeding and background among the officers themselves. I don't know how you translate it, so I think that a film that presents this problem, very often, in my terms, in my Puritanical, if you like, and severe terms of language convention, ought not to be dubbed, unless equivalents can be found. Anyway, I don't violate this convention any more. In the case of that particular picture, it was done, and I think it lessens its credibility considerably.

"The picture was, again, a melodrama. It had Paul Muni, who was not at home at all in Europe, and who was unhappy every moment of the time he was there, and who seemed to have no curiosity about the place where he was. True, he was at a very critical time in his life, and it was very strange for him, as it was for me.

"It has been said that the picture was a foreigner's and particularly an American's look at Italy, and that's true. I'd never been in Italy before. It was a country that I'd stayed away from because of Mussolini, my distaste for Mussolini, and, therefore, when I went to Europe for the first time after the war, in 1951, to do this film, it was my first visit to Italy, and many things struck me with an incredible force, and they're evoked, and perhaps exaggerated, in the film. I think much of it is pretty overcrowded photographically, and I think there are excellent acting performances, and the script originally had considerable merit. It was based on an original story by Noël Calef, who was around then, and who's become a great friend of mine. He is an Italian-born Frenchman, and he always disapproved of the script and of the film. We've remained friends in spite of that. The rights have reverted to him, and I believe that he has asked that all versions of it be destroyed, but, as I say, I have heard that recently the film has been shown, so I don't think he's been successful. It's a film that I cannot any longer care about, and which I think was certainly a failure from anybody's point of view."

"*A foreigner's vision of a country is often more accurate than the native's.*"

"Well, that's true, but then that has to be an observation of *that* country, and we had a number of Italians who were playing in English, which they had learned phonetically but which they didn't understand. It was impossible to have any close contact with them. Their delivery of the lines was slow, and, of course, they weren't being Italians, they were being Italians speaking English. We had Paul Muni, whose nationality was not identified, we had Joan Lorring, who was very American, very Brooklyn American, and it became a *mélange*, the whole thing was a *mélange*, the producers were half Italian and half American, the writers were American, the capital was French, one of the actresses was French, two American actors, and an American director. It was a mess."

"*I was thinking more perhaps of your view of England.*"

"Well, I think that's true, and I think that my view of Italy, or perhaps other countries, might now be interesting too, but I would then want to present French people as French, or deal with Americans or English people in those settings, but not have them pretending to be the real thing, unless it was a picture that completely departed from reality — realism, naturalism — and was using a highly stylised technique, then perhaps it's possible. For example, I very much want to do *Galileo* as a film. *Galileo* has to be shot in

Italy. One would never get the money for it as a strictly Italian film, and what I would try to do would be to shoot it in Italy, on the original locations, selecting, however, what I chose to show, in highly stylised fashion, and make no pretence that the language was Italian, but treat it almost as a theatre production."

"I've heard some interesting stories about how Galileo *was translated."*

"In a sense it was written in English because, though it entirely existed in German, I don't think it had had a German production, and Laughton and Brecht worked on it for quite a long time in English, trying to get an English version. I came in about three months before that was completed. I participated in it, so it became a three-way business of Brecht, Laughton and myself on the script in English. Then, when Brecht left, the last scene was not satisfactory to him, or to any of us for that matter, and I brought in George Tabori. Brecht left me fairly copious notes about what he thought was wrong with the last scene, and we had discussions, and from these notes and through the discussions between Tabori, Laughton and myself the last scene was re-written so that the scene as it was played in New York was different from what it was in Hollywood. By the way, Brecht apparently approved of all this very much, and I also did add certain things about the staging at the beginning and the end, such as the reading of some of the *Discorsi* of Galileo, which were not in the original. All of this Brecht saw photographically, and he read the script, and he heard about it from all of us, and approved, and I believe these ideas have been incorporated since in his German version of the play. I've heard that he himself re-wrote after this for the German production. There is some talk of doing it over here on the stage, quite apart from a film version, and I'd still love to do the stage version because I don't think it has been done properly here." *Joseph Losey* (J.D.L.)

I suppose I feel that, whether or not Losey himself worries much about the fate of *Stranger on the Prowl*, it is obviously a work of interest to myself and other critics, and that its total suppression or destruction would be unfortunate. One can sympathise with a writer such as Calef, who feels that the film betrays the vision he expressed in his medium, but a film, after all, is the product of the work of other people — writers, a director — with other visions of the world, and almost inevitably it must alter, or "betray" the vision of the work on which it is based.

One would have thought that a Losey production of Brecht's *Galileo Galilei* would be precisely what the National Theatre or Lincoln Center should be offering us; it might well be the theatrical event of the sixties.

8. The Sleeping Tiger

"**W**E THOUGHT the script itself was frightful, and it embarrassed us incredibly to do it. Joe had to embellish this rubbish, as he always has had to do, and in consequence it was much more exciting to do: one found reasons for doing dreadful dialogue, and making it sound alright." *Dirk Bogarde* (I.S.)

In *The Sleeping Tiger*, Losey uses the genre of the domestic melodrama (hard-working husband married to the wrong woman: "All ice on the outside. Rotten inside.") to re-work some of the themes that have already appeared in his American movies (particularly *M* and *The Big Night*). He works with the genre, not trying to make melodramatic climaxes acceptable by toning them down with realistic underplaying; thus the genre achieves its own alienation effect: the audience laughs at the melodramatic cliché, and thus unconsciously rejects the assumptions and oversimplifications of human behaviour upon which the genre is based. This Losey wants it to do. However, Losey is doing more than merely mocking the genre: the genre of film melodrama bears precisely the same relationship to the audience's life and frustrations that the characters' sometimes melodramatic behaviour bears to their lives and frustrations. People, society in general, turn to the melodrama out of dissatisfaction. As always with Losey, one must beware of the easy response, the simple answer. Those who are too ready to laugh miss an essential point: passion in excess, passion which can find no suitable channels or outlets, inevitably becomes somewhat ridiculous, just as melodrama is ridiculous. Yet it is no answer to reject passion: Losey always leaves the spectator to form his own conclusions about the characters he presents; there is very real force in Glenda Esmond's description of her cool, shrewd, calculating psychiatrist husband as "The man who could perform miracles, but couldn't keep his wife."

Clive Esmond succeeds in reforming the young delinquent Frank Clements partly because he is able to keep himself from getting emotionally involved in their relationship. He is always the doctor, nagging away at the background underlying Frank's criminality, refusing to show anger or jealousy; permissive, but only in as much as he does not side with society in punishing Frank. His work is his passion, and so his marriage to Glenda can never be something in which he is intensely involved; his secretary/receptionist, Carol, would obviously be a far more suitable wife. Significantly, he and Glenda have no children. With Glenda, he is still a doctor; when their relationship is about to break down, she turns on him: "Don't prescribe for me ... You nag." The marriage may once have been satisfactory for Glenda, who was fleeing from the background of a broken home, and a mother who hated her, to try to find security and build a life for herself. She admires Clive's power, and he is an important man in his society. However, Frank's intrusion immediately provokes a conflict in her feelings which is expressed in her attitude towards Frank and Clive's first encounter, when Frank tried to hold Clive up at gun-point: she is fascinated both by her husband's skill at judo, which enabled him to disarm Frank, and by Frank's violence: "Would you have used that gun on Clive?" she asks. Frank quickly senses all the passions she has denied herself. "You're a phoney. You're a tight wire," he tells her.

She responds to Frank with a hostility (though she accuses him of rudeness, she is far more rude than he is) that quickly turns to a fascinated attraction. Part of this hostility has been displaced on to Frank from Clive, who has brought his experiment, his work, into their very household without consulting her. She, in turn, provokes a complex of emotions in Frank. She is like his hated step-mother. Thus, by seducing her, Frank would get his revenge on Glenda, for her hostility, on his step-mother, his father, and on Clive, who, as his analyst, is automatically cast in the role of his father, and who, by disarming him during their first encounter, and then giving him the choice of being his guinea-pig, or being turned over to the police, establishes a fairly loose parental authority over him.

Thus, the central triangle of the plot of the movie is, essentially, the central triangle of the "plot" of most neuroses, and — given the Freudian displacements that Frank naturally makes in this situation — Frank first acts out, then works through a fantasy shared by many neurotic patients. He changes as he gets involved with both Clive and Glenda; at first he says his step-mother was a fine woman, but he becomes restless and walks about under questioning. When Clive has taken his side in an interview with the policeman Inspector Simmons (another authority figure who resembles Clive in appearance), Frank admits his mother didn't die, "She ran away." "You hated your father. Why?"; "Because he made my mother leave him." Frank's step-mother was "All ice on the outside. Rotten inside." "How did you get even with them?" Clive asks, unaware that Frank is about to gain his revenge now, through the relationship with Glenda; already she has asked him eagerly to come riding with her again, and when Clive rejects her suggestion that they have dinner together (as usual, he has a meeting), she goes out with Frank. There are several slightly perverse overtones to this relationship: Glenda's fascination with violence is linked with a desire to be humiliated, cheapened, become a possession, like one of the women Frank once suggested he might bring to the house (this image of Frank's girls is *her* invention; when she implies that her taste in clothes is somewhat finer than that of the girls Frank normally associates with, he rounds on her to defend his friends: "They read *Vogue* magazine, too. They just don't happen to have so much money." She apologises: "Expensive dress. Cheap remark." "Go upstairs and put on something a little cheaper," Frank replies. A few moments later she is made up to resemble her image of a tart). Once Frank has established a relationship with Glenda, his guilt forces him to resist Clive's analysis. He seeks to play with Glenda, to demonstrate his power; he kisses her when Clive is in the house, and ignores her when they return to the basement club he frequents in Soho, thus provoking her into a hysterical car-drive and outburst of tears; her passions, once so repressed, are now starting to run dangerously out of control.

Clive is puzzled by his failure with Frank. When Bailey, the fiancé of the maid, Sally, whom Frank terrorised into leaving her job, comes to the house, Clive gives him a long lecture on the virtues of psycho-analysis, and then buys him off with a fat cheque. (Sally strongly resembled Glenda Esmond in appearance; Frank had not then achieved any real power over Glenda, and so his revenge on Glenda, for her insults, and on his step-mother, could only be taken on Sally, who was lower than he in the pecking-order — displacement again). The "message" content of the lecture is admirably "placed" by the surrounding action: the sophisticated audience which laughs at or rejects this "preaching" (as some do) is just failing to respond to the subtlety of the movie. Losey neither expects an audience to be converted to the virtues of psycho-analysis by Clive's speech, nor does he show Bailey being converted: Bailey has come for money (if he weren't after money, he'd have gone straight to the police); Clive knows he has come for money, and Bailey knows that Clive knows. The "lecture" is just a formality or routine preliminary to the financial transaction, a ritual that must be observed, and the financial transaction subtly qualifies the positives put forward by the "lecture" (and thus those presented by the film; there are, though, other things at work in the film that undermine the positive attitude to psycho-analysis that, at first glance, it seems to present; for example, our attitude toward Clive, the analyst).

Still Frank does not respond; he comes down at night, and searches for Clive's cheque-book to confirm his suspicions: "You bribed him to bribe me ... You can't buy me." Demonstrating his independence, he goes out the next day with a gun, and holds up and robs an office. Simultaneously, we see that Clive has reached the point where he can see no hope of progress with Frank. Carol, his secretary, tells him: "It's no good. An experiment that went wrong. Give it up and forget it." Ostensibly she is talking about the attempt to cure Frank, but something in her manner, plus the insight into the nature of displacement that the movie has already revealed, make it clear that she is really talking about Clive's marriage to Glenda.

The necessary emotional breakthrough with Frank is precipitated by a second visit from Inspector Simmons, who is pretty sure he will be able to prove that Frank committed the hold-up. Frank has no alibi, but Clive states firmly: "Frank was with me all afternoon."

TIME WITHOUT PITY:
"You don't know what it's like to be left alone."
David Graham (Michael Redgrave) and Robert Stanford (Leo McKern).

THE GYPSY AND THE GENTLEMAN:
destructive violence rather than constructive action.

BLIND DATE exposes the illusions of a whole society, from the self-deceiving establishment downwards. Above, Jan (Hardy Kruger) in Parliament Square, surrounded by traditional symbols of British democracy and public service.

BLIND DATE. Above (right): Jan's ability to create is limited by his background. He can paint old age or the struggles of the miners but not female beauty. Jan and his Jacqueline (Micheline Presle).

BLIND DATE: Morgan can see only a tart's flat, belonging to the kind of woman who "can drive a man half out of his senses". Westover (John Van Eyssen), Morgan (Stanley Baker), and Jan (Hardy Kruger).

"Have you considered that a conviction for perjury would ruin you?" Simmons asks. Having committed himself, Clive does not back out, and Simmons leaves without being able to make an arrest. Left alone with Clive, Frank breaks down and recounts the childhood trauma underlying his criminal behaviour; as in *M*, there was a punishment for theft, a theft provoked by an unjust action — Frank's father had confiscated the money Frank had saved: "I wanted to kill him . . . It was my money . . . I went out and stole one . . . 'Justice,' he said, 'must be done' . . . he twisted my arm and made me kneel down in front of her, and then he beat me . . . A week later he was dead." Frank's step-mother got drunk, and accused him: "You killed him"; Frank admits "I prayed for it." Like M, Frank wanted to be punished. The motifs of arm-twisting and falling, of looking up at an aggressor, occur throughout the film, until Frank's account explains their significance: Clive twists Frank's arm to disarm him; he stands looking down on him at their first analytical session; Frank throws Sally to the floor.

Once this crisis is past, Frank turns away from Glenda to spend all his time with Clive, till finally he no longer needs Clive either. After a trip to the country, Frank stays on alone fishing while Clive goes back to Glenda, and he then comes to the decision that he must give himself up to the police. Glenda cannot accept the rejection this involves: "You're not going to give me notice, like a servant or a waitress" (her pre-occupation with class is continually fused into her attitude towards sex), and her hatred of both Frank and Clive breaks out uncontrollably. She drives her car (with Frank in it) through a giant Esso poster of a springing tiger, and dies in the wreck. Clive is left with Carol, and Frank survives the accident to surrender to Inspector Simmons, and thus free himself from his past. The resolution of the film is not the simple "commercial" for psycho-analysis that at first sight it may seem to be; though Clive has "cured" Frank, it is very clear that he needed Frank, and, in a sense, used him to solve his own emotional and marital problems; just as Clive frees Frank from the legacy of his past, so Frank frees Clive from Glenda, his past. It is true, certainly, that Frank, whose character contains a fusion of certain traits of both M and George La Main, is presented as educable, redeemable. He is freed from his compulsions, and learns how to accept responsibility for his actions. Thus, Clive is vindicated, yet Clive never truly sees, let alone accepts, his responsibility for the failure of his marriage. There are no simple answers.

9. The Intimate Stranger

R EGGIE Wilson is an American film-editor who has been forced to leave Hollywood as a result of a scandal involving a married woman. He has come over to England, "made a winner" with his first picture as an executive, and married the boss's daughter. However he has not yet understood his past, his responsibilities to other people, or achieved real security. His story is narrated in flashback (he is recounting his problems to a doctor); he comments on his marriage: "I loved Lesley. Not that I hadn't used people in the past." He feels that his new career in a new country, and his marriage, represent a complete break with the past, but they don't. He has persuaded someone from his past, Kay Wallace, a big star with whom he once had a love-affair, to come over to England as he needs her for his new film, an ambitious large-budget project. In their first conversation, it is clear that Kay is a bit unsure of the relationship that Reggie wishes to establish with her; she wonders how Lesley will feel about meeting her; Reggie replies: "I'm married to the one woman in the world who'll understand." She tells him: "This time, don't throw it away. In Hollywood, you're still on the bad boys' list." Then she asks: "Are you really married?" He knows exactly what she means, in terms of his attitude toward life and women, but he convinces her of his love for Lesley, and assures her that she and Lesley are going to be great friends; he tells her: "You're a friend; almost like old times"; Kay replies with a tinge of sadness and bitterness: "Almost." Later, when things have started to go wrong, Kay rounds on him for trading on her past affection to lure her over to England to get "his precious picture done." The evidence is presented objectively: Kay is disappointed that his love for her is dead, and this is reinforced by the fact that she believes he has not thrown her over for a wife whom he really loves, but is still running around with movie-studio camp-followers. Reggie seems truly to respect Kay and want her friendship, but Kay probably has some justification for feeling hurt and disappointed; it seems to have been insensitive of him not to realise Kay might still love him.

The crisis in Reggie's life is precipitated by the arrival of a series of letters from an American girl, Evelyn, who claims to have had a passionate affair with him. Reggie does not know her, but she aggravates his underlying emotional insecurity: when he shows the first letter to his wife Lesley he is pathetically tense. Later, Lesley has to tell him "I'm not a judge. You don't have to collect witnesses to build up a case." At the same time, the new film, *Eclipse*, is running into trouble; Reggie is forced to oppose Ben, his father-in-law, who regrets he has outgrown the day of the low-budget movie, and at the same time turn to him for help over the letters. There are problems, too, about the ending of the movie: about whether a man who has made a mistake should have another chance. The round table discussion about the movie gives a beautifully concise image of the movie-business: a group of rather dull, boring, not very intelligent businessmen discussing what they want the movie to say: "Leave the question open"; "Then why charge them admission?"; "We've got to make up our minds one way or another." It is not that these men irresponsibly exploit their audience — in fact, they seem very aware of their responsibilities — just that they obviously have nothing to say. Reggie, for example, seems incapable of seeing any relationship between his own predicament, and that of the character in his movie.

Reggie is dragged deeper into the nightmare, until he admits "Either I'm crazy, or everybody else is." The picture has been taken off the schedule; Lesley believes Evelyn's letters (after an unsuccessful attempt at a showdown with Evelyn, Reggie has compromised himself by kissing her: "I was in a mood to find out just how far she would go."). He turns to Kay for help, and she suggests he take medical advice, but the doctor, too, is unable to help him. Reggie is due to leave the studios, ostensibly for a trip. With his life collapsed around him, he thinks for a moment of suicide, then suddenly sees Evelyn (who has sent all her letters from Newcastle) walking through the studios: he, and the audience, suddenly glimpse the possibility of a way out of this situation, which has become so entangled that it seemed there could be no resolution. The moment has some of the power of that magnificent instant in *Blind Date* when Jan catches sight of his Jacqueline at London Airport.

Though Evelyn has come to try to blackmail Ben, whom she believes to be behind the plot against Reggie, she is forced into a showdown in a dubbing studio with Ernie Chaple, Ben's closest associate, who had paid her money to write the letters to Reggie. The conversation is overheard over the sound equipment, and Reggie's name cleared. After this dénouement, there is a moment which states one of the movie's essential themes; Evelyn flirtatiously asks Reggie: "Haven't got a match, have you?" and he automatically flirts back as he lights her cigarette; then, as she walks away, he realises what has happened, and says: "I guess I had Evelyn Stewart coming to me." He has learnt something: though he had

68

not in fact known Evelyn in the past, she is the type of many girls whom he had known, and the cigarette-lighting incident evokes with beautiful precision the kind of relationship he had with them. Just as Evelyn is an embodiment of his past affairs, the impotent Ernie Chaple (Evelyn taunts him: "I bet you never had a girl in your life"), perched up high, in god-like command of the dubbing-studio, is a comment on the lovelessness of his former relation-ships, the use he has made of people to further his projects, and the sterility of his attitude towards the cinema: certain character traits in the normal Reggie, when heightened to an extreme in Ernie, form the basis of Ernie's pathological condition.

10. Time Without Pity

"WHEN I first came to England, I worked under extremely forced conditions of budget, subject and schedule. Some-times these restrictions help, sometimes the film inevitably suffers . . . I have been accused of overloading my films. Under the conditions which I had to work with, it is quite probable I crammed some of the films too full of the things that were important to me." *Joseph Losey* (J.B.)

"As a social document, it runs out of ink. But as a thriller it is first-rate." *Philip Oakes*[4]

"Here time itself becomes man's ultimate prison, and the 'race against time' of thriller tradition takes on the significance of a metaphysical principle." *Robin Wood*[5]

One of the peculiar forces of Losey's art derives from the tension

[4] *Evening Standard* 21.3.57 quoted as a National Film Theatre programme note, Spring 1966.
[5] *Motion* No. 4 February 1963. This is unquestionably one of the finest pieces of Losey criticism, and is on an entirely different level from many of its com-panion pieces in this *Companion to Violence and Sadism in the Cinema*.

which exists between the genre in which he is working and the logic of the structure and symbolism of his movie. His films have a formal coherence of meaning on more than one level. Thus films like *The Boy with Green Hair*, *The Lawless*, and *M*, which ostensibly treat radically different social problems (war, racialism, society's attitude to and responsibility for the criminal psychopath) are united by the fact that each evokes the atmosphere of a witch-hunt; as the era of the McCarthyite hysteria nears, so the society Losey depicts becomes more uncontrollably hysterical. *The Boy* and *M* are also linked, entirely appropriately, by the thread of highly delicate Freudian imagery that runs through each.

On one level, *Time Without Pity*, an adaptation of Emlyn Williams's play *Someone Waiting*, a revenge melodrama of questionable merit, in which the action takes place after the execution of the innocent young man, is a protest movie, aimed at the evils of capital punishment, and the individual's indifference to this evil. David Graham, desperate to save his son Alec, whom he is convinced is innocent, visits an anti-hanging M.P. and a crusading anti-hanging journalist, seeking help. The M.P. is not much interested in Alec's possible innocence, only in his general crusade to do away with capital punishment. Our sympathy is strongly with David (Losey showed us the murder and the murderer, Stanford, at the beginning of the movie; there is no attempt, *à la* Dearden, to "sugar the pill" of a social problem by tacking it, and some "message" speeches, on to the framework of a "who really dun it"), and we share his frustrated disappointment with the M.P.'s lack of concern. Later, the journalist, whom David has known for a long time, says: "Why should I help you? . . . There were other fathers and other sons." David, by his apathy, has condoned the injustice of the system. Just as David has shirked his responsibilities as a member of society, so he has shirked his responsibilities in his private life — as a father. Despite David's neglect, Alec has always retained his love for his father, his hope that one day David will write a great novel; David has even been cast in the role of a father-figure by Brian Stanford. Thus David's alcoholism is a symbol, in a heightened way, of apathy toward the problems and responsibilities of life in general, half symbol, half symptom of a general social malaise. He is no less reprehensible than Agnes Cole, who rounds on him: "Your son killed my sister, and I'm glad he's going to die."

Alec Graham, in turn, is a symbol, in a heightened way, of all humanity: like Alec, we are all under sentence of death; death is the one certain fact about any human existence. But Alec has had no real opportunity to live a meaningful existence; he has been swept away and submerged in a tumult of emotional conflicts which he has hardly been able properly to understand, let alone control. One inevitably links his predicament with his father's inadequacies; there is a sense, too, in which one may interpret Alec's situation as particularly symbolic of his generation, threatened with nuclear war.

Alec's impending execution, then, and its general symbolic significance, give a perspective to the action of the film, reminding us of our common humanity, as does the title of the film; connected with this complex of symbols is the character of Mrs. Harker: she and her daughter Vicky may be able to help David (Vicky was a close friend of the murdered girl), but have been bought off. Mrs. Harker lives in a room surrounded by clocks; her hobby is an expression of a pathological preoccupation with the passing of time; it is almost as if she wished magically to subject time to her control. David Graham, too, is continually conscious of the passing of time, naturally enough, as he has arrived in England from a sanitorium for alcoholics with barely 24 hours left in which to find proof of his son's innocence; he looks repeatedly at clocks or at his watch, He has been forced back into life, and time takes on a heightened significance for him: he feels he has only these 24 hours in which to establish the meaningfulness of his own existence by saving his son — all that survives from the wreck he has made of his life. Thus David Graham, too, stands in a heightened way for all humanity.

Stanford, the self-made man, industrialist and mechanic, rich, energetic and powerful (physically and socially) is equally obsessed with the necessity to establish a meaning in his life — dominating, bullying, driving others, wishing to control people as he can the cars he designs. His loveless mariage, to a woman from a better social background who has certain intellectual pretensions, is a source of continual irritation and tension to him. He is trapped and goaded (like the bull in the Goya on the wall of his apartment) by the position in society he has carved out for himself, and can achieve communication only with his cars: the trial run he takes in his new model is a terrifying image of frustrated sexuality finding its expression in *power*. He is drawn irresistibly to David Graham by unconscious forces of which he has no comprehension: Stanford, obsessed with the idea of control, is himself the person over whom he has least control, as the murder he committed at the start of the film makes clear. Perhaps he wants to keep an eye on Graham; he wishes to dominate, destroy even, the failure whose son is about to die for the murder he has committed; there is a tinge of compassion, or perhaps almost self-pitying identification with Graham — both are alone — though, on the conscious level, Stanford sees only his own loneliness: "You don't know what it's like to be alone," he says, then adds suspiciously, "How drunk are you?" He talks of "big decisions" that a man must carry "alone for the rest of his life." He has had a realisation of himself that is intolerable; he, Stanford, is what Hargreaves becomes as a result of his final action in *King and Country*. Losey says of Hargreaves: "At the moment when that bullet is fired, he's dead. I mean it's no

longer going to be possible for that man to hide from himself . . .
it may be for certain hours, and days and weeks, but it will come
back in the night, and it will come back with a shock, suddenly in
a conversation, and it's there." (J.D.L.) Graham's alcoholism and
the idea of escape now fascinate Stanford: "Drink," he says, "Can
black out everything"; Graham replies: "It can't black out the
man with the rope." Ultimately, though, his fascination with
Graham is an expression of the twin forces that dominate and
control his life: guilt and destructive aggression. He wants Graham
to know that he is the murderer; guilt is forcing him to confession;
at the same time, if Graham knows that Stanford is the killer, but
yet is still unable to save his son from the man with the rope,
Stanford will have achieved the ultimate in control: complete
mastery, the reduction of another human being to utter helplessness.

Through his relationship with Stanford, Graham discovers that
release (not just a temporary release of tension, but permanent
release from the problems of existence) is the inevitable end of his
mission if it is to be successful: he can only save the son who needs
him by giving up his own life, and thus implicating Stanford. In
fact, the 24 hours Alec had left to live prove to be the 24 hours of
life left to David his father. In a sense they are his *whole* life, on account of his previous evasion through alcoholism (in Losey's
work, the peace of escapism is very close to the peace of death). It
is a comment on the nature of his previous life that the only gesture
of affirmation of which he is capable is to die to preserve his son,
who had needed him before, and whom he has failed before.
Alec's zombie-like protective shell at the start of the movie is a
defence against the idea of death, and against his need for the
father who has so often failed him. For the prison official, it is
something desirable, protecting Alec from the reality of his situation.
Alec's emotional unfreezing, which makes genuine communication

73

possible in his second interview with his father ("I don't want to die. Please save me") is something of which, given their task, they cannot approve — an expression of life. David, by himself, had been unable to give his life meaning, but he does find both meaning and peace as he dies in Stanford's arms. In his unique case, suicide is a positive act as well as being his final evasion.

11. The Gypsy and the Gentleman

"TO TELL you the truth, I was so upset about *The Gypsy and the Gentleman* after it was shot that it's the only film I've ever made where I just turned over the score and the dubbing to someone else." *Joseph Losey* (J.D.L.)

Though *Gypsy and the Gentleman* is very far from being the movie Losey planned and wanted to make, it has the formal coherence and stylistic consistency that is the signature of his work: it is a Losey film, an interesting film, complex thematically, an important film even, though not a great film. Losey never judges a film of his by what it achieves, but only by what he set out to achieve when he started to make it. Thus he very much underrates films like *The Gypsy and the Gentleman*, or even the Hakim version of *Eve*, because they represent a compromise or betrayal of his intentions, and thus of his deepest feelings and concerns. For the critic or viewer who is sensitive to Losey's art, such films, though imperfect, are memorable because he is able to respond to the concern that determines their formal pattern: they are successful on a level so intense and profound that certain glaring surface flaws or imperfections no longer matter; one is willing to write these flaws off as failures of technique rather than any kind of artistic or aesthetic failure. But Losey is as deeply a technician as he is an artist: for him technical perfection is a necessary condition for artistic greatness, something without which what might have been a profound insight into the human condition can become mere pretentiousness: "The selected reality-symbol must be perfect." Thus he has an especial love for a film like *The Servant*, over which he had complete control, and in which everything *works*.

In *The Gypsy and the Gentleman*, for perhaps the first time, Losey suggests the presence of some kind of fate or destiny at work, drawing Deverill and Belle inevitably together; this is expressed through both cutting and the construction of the image. Losey cuts from Deverill just about to leave his revels in London to the gypsy pair Belle and Jess in the country, then back to Deverill and Vanessa's father in the coach discussing Deverill's possible marriage to Vanessa (Deverill says he does not love Vanessa, but "I'll treat her well"; her father hopes she will turn him into a responsible master of his property); Losey then cuts to a long-shot of the coach travelling along the road; as it passes, Jess and Belle come into frame. Some time later Jess, who has noticed that Belle attracts Deverill, arranges that Belle should stop Deverill's coach in the rain: "I've lost my way, sir"; "And found it again, it seems," Deverill replies, amused, stepping immediately into the trap Jess has baited for him. Jess and Belle have lighted upon the Deverill estate through chance, or fate, but Jess then takes charge, coldly and unemotionally manupulating his mistress Belle and her relationship with Deverill so that she will be able to extract as much from Deverill as possible. Jess shapes his own destiny, and that of Belle, who loves him, and would do anything for him, and that of the weak and pliable Deverill, for whom Belle is a perfect complement. "The Deverill women have always been stronger than the men," he has told Vanessa when proposing to her, an interesting admission, because Deverill, sportsman, gambler, philanderer — "The woman's not been born who can put the cap and bells on me," he tells his sister — is the very image of what is superficially considered to be masculine strength.

Jess, emotionless, needing nobody, is able to control people as Stanford controls his cars. After her first night with Deverill, Belle returns to Jess. She wants him, physically. "Kiss me," she says; "What pickings?" he asks; she gives him a purse of money she has stolen: "There's more to come"; Jess: "Unless he tires. Men do"; Belle: "Not Deverill. He'll need me more each day," then: "Do you need me, pig man?"; Jess: "No." Later, when their position is threatened, Jess warns Belle: "If I run, I run alone." Jess's self-sufficiency attracts her, just as hers attracts Deverill. Belle uses Deverill just as Jess uses her; though Deverill may have dominated his other women, he allows himself, almost wants to be dominated by Belle. He only crosses her over Hattie, the maid who is his illegitimate child, though Belle has to deceive him about some aspects of her treatment of his sister. Hattie, in turn, is sensitive to the nuances of the power-struggle, being rude to Belle and flirting with Jess when she feels she is safe. This world, precisely because its members are inward-looking, obsessed with power and status rather than genuine achievement, is to some extent ultimately self-destructive. Those who survive are those, like Sarah and John, who do have some genuine purpose in life, or those such as Jess, who are utterly ruthless in every relationship, and make no kind of emotional or sentimental contact with others. There is something essentially Darwinian about this aspect of Losey's vision, which allows characters like Jess to survive, and Belle and Deverill to die. Inherited wealth, position or influence may insulate the individual from the struggle for survival, but such an inheritance can easily be dissipated, and the individual who suddenly loses his protection, and who is left to defend himself by his own efforts and personality, is faced with a struggle which is usually too much for him. This is true of the debt-ridden Deverill; it is also true of Tony in *The Servant*. Luxury has made them unfitted for a place in the real worlds of struggle and conflict, or of creation and enterprise. Both characters may be taken as symbols of a certain kind of failure or desire to live in the past (Deverill says wistfully of a bottle of wine: "My father brought it back from Burgundy when he was a young man. There was a king in France then.") that is of immediate relevance to the present state of Britain. Emotions, too, even positive ones, are a weakness for those who are trapped in this Darwinian world, perhaps because they cannot be controlled. Like Belle, Jan's Jacqueline in *Blind Date* and Bannion in *The Criminal* are both destroyed as a result of expressing or attempting to express their emotions: at the climax of this film, Deverill decides to drown himself and Belle rather than save Belle from drowning (which was his original intention) because she wants Jess; she calls after Jess. "You're safe now, you're safe," Deverill tells her; "Not without Jess," she replies, "let me go to Jess, let me go." Losey's art expresses a mistrust of the emotions, which are usually obsessional and destructive rather than healthy and constructive: attraction is seldom a matter of innate sympathy and response; it may involve intense sexual excitement but seldom profound sexual communication. Losey has said: "For me, anyway, this is certain: there is a deliverance through the intellect, but not through emotion." (C.L.)

Though Losey is obviously far more involved in the Deverill/Belle/Jess triangle, there are certain memorable touches in his handling of the relationship between Deverill, his sister Sarah, and her lover John. Deverill rejects John as a suitor for Sarah because he is poor, and is a professional man: "She'll stay a maid till she's 21," he tells John, "Find yourself another sawbones, and wed his sister." Deverill's treatment of John is similar to his servants' treatment of the gypsies. John's pride, and his desire to succeed through his own efforts, alienate him from Sarah for a time. At

77

Belle's instigation, the corruptible lawyer Brook gives Sarah false information about her late aunt's will (Deverill blinds himself to many of Belle's activities; his refusal to accept the guilt that much money-making inevitably involves is typical of his class). Brook tells Sarah she will only receive her inheritance if she waits till she is 21 before marrying. Sarah decides to obey her aunt's wishes not so much because she wants the money but because she knew and trusted her aunt. Her decision is very hurtful to John, who tells her: "Very well, be an heiress. But be it alone." Though a craft or profession confers a stigma in aristocratic society, it is an expression of some kind of genuine identity and purpose in life. The "Game Pup," Deverill's prize-fighter, is tempted by the money in fighting, but when Deverill accuses him of wanting to be paid twice for a fight (Belle has stolen the purse Deverill left for him) he replies "I'll not sell my good name for a purse." John's knowledge helps to free him partially from the crippling restraints of a hierarchical society: he helps Mrs. Haggard, a legendary actress whose skill has made her, too, to some extent classless. She in turn, helps him, and she ultimately is able to save Sarah from the private bedlam to which Deverill has committed her by drunkenly signing a paper without reading its contents, because her fame has given her friends in high places. Mrs. Haggard is successful, thus she can afford to be good, but even she is implicated in the general complicity: she has a negro page-boy whom she treats as a toy or pet, despite her affection for him. Though her actions are motivated by good, there is some parallel between her success and Belle's strivings: in their different ways, they use their innate qualities to rise in society, and achieve freedom. No other way is left open to them. There is, however, this vital difference: Mrs. Haggard's place in society depends, ultimately, upon her own personality or sense of identity; it is the result of skill, training and hardwork, a creative preoccupation. Belle attempts to establish her identity by means of obtaining a place in society: she talks always of her noble father, who seduced and abandoned her mother, a dream-figure which underlines her lack of identity, the fact that she belongs nowhere, not even with the gypsies, who "never rear the half-child." Once Belle has obtained some power, she uses it to obtain vengeance. Jess uses the money she has gotten for him to barter for a gypsy wife; Belle, now Lady Deverill, drives the group of gypsies off her land. They retaliate by raiding the house, slashing pictures and destroying ornaments, an outburst rather similar to that displayed by Belle herself when she learned that she'd "married a pack of bills, and a mortgaged house" — destructive violence rather than constructive action: master, servant, slave, outsider, all accept the basic social structure, trying to manipulate it to their own good; breaking down into outbursts of frustrated rage when their efforts fail.

12. Blind Date

"**B**RISK and well-made if illogical whodunit, laced with sex, class feeling and hints of corruption at Scotland Yard." *Sight and Sound.*[6]

"*Blind Date*, I would say, was, in a certain way, a transition period. It was the last and best of one kind, and it foreshadowed another kind . . .

"When we got into *Blind Date*, I felt it essential, because it was a very unrealistic story — a very trite story, and a rather incredible story in terms of contrivance — that we give it as much interest in terms of observation and reality as we could, and that the characters be very rich. Therefore, I wanted to make the artist a coal-miner, and somebody who was self-made and still painted from the

[6] *Sight and Sound*, Summer-Autumn 1959.

memory of his earlier experiences, and I wanted to use Stanley as a Welshman who, as I've already said, is a natural antagonist to the English — I don't know whether the outside world understands this or not — and who was also working-class, but who found himself caught up in a British class-structure of the most rigid old boy kind of set-up, where, unless he behaved in certain ways, his chances of promotion were slight, but who shared with the Dutchman a kind of passionate sense and desire for the truth. The truth that the boy knew was one thing, the truth that Morgan saw was another, because he saw a tart's flat. And we tried to make a flat that had, in fact, three layers: first of all it had been a stable on an old estate, and there are elements of that stable; secondly, it had probably been lived in by a series of people who were rather tasteless and bourgeois, the last layer of which was the decoration that the girl herself had probably carried out, with the money of her lover. And the third one consisted of the few very valuable things that he'd given her, like that genuine small van Dyck, which in fact it was, and a few other things. So that, to a very careful observer, there were three layers. However, Morgan would see only a tart's flat, the Dutchman would see none of this, except the girl he knew, or thought he knew, excepting perhaps these very valuable things, which he couldn't reconcile with the interior of this flat."

"It upset people; they seemed to want to reject what the film was saying, and started to talk about hints of corruption at Scotland Yard, and so on; that's not really the right word, is it?"

"No, it's influence, knowing the right people. Being the right person. Doing the right thing. It did upset people, but not everybody, by any means, and now it's very old hat. I don't think that there's anything in *Blind Date* that would shock anybody now, but at the time it was different. John Trevelyan had just become censor. He wasn't at all disturbed by that aspect of it. He was very worried about one dressing, or rather, undressing, scene, which he cut, I

THE CRIMINAL. Top, Bannion (Stanley Baker) who is "big, inside", and Scout (Jack Rodney), who's been there so long "he's forgotten they did away with the no-talking rule." Centre, a party in Bannion's flat – Bannion never truly frees himself from the prison. At left, the prison governor knows he's beaten and just goes through the motions of being a humanitarian – Barrows (Patrick Magee), Bannion (Stanley Baker) and the Governor (Noel Willman).

THE CRIMINAL: "*Don't let that* thing *touch me.*"
Mike Carter (Sam Wanamaker), Maggie (Jill Bennett), and Bannion (Stanley Baker).

THE DAMNED:
King (Oliver Reed)
is frightened by the
vision of violence he
sees in the statues
of Freya (Viveca
Lindfors).
"They're nasty,
that's what."

think mistakenly, but it's the only time he has cut anything out of any film of mine. The people who were distributing it, in particular, and some of the people who had a part of the financing, were very concerned about the attitude toward the police, which they hadn't encountered before (and which they thought was part of the job of the censorship): that it was not in good taste, that it was not true, and so on. As a matter of fact, I think that the Baker character is highly flattering to the police, and the question of influence is not likely to affect only the English. It occurs wherever somebody knows somebody else, on whatever basis you can get to speak to him. Not to ask him to be dishonest, necessarily, in return for any favour, but just to suggest that certain kinds of behaviour are not advantageous, and that others are. This bothered them, of course. Then, I suppose, the suggestion that a high-ranking diplomat was involved in a sexual scandal. This now has, of course, become rather old hat. But this attitude is typical of most film industries. It's certainly typical of the American industry, and it's pretty much typical of the English industry . . . And to suggest that there could be real characters and a certain minimal of content in a thriller was virtually heresy. Although there had been a few adult thrillers before, there hadn't been any adult treatment of the English police system. Curiously enough, in this respect the Americans are much more liberal. They, people in general, don't like the police in the United States. It's largely taken for granted that a certain percentage of them are corrupt, and *The Prowler*, which presented a man who was pathetic, and if you like eventually psychopathic, and who was a victim to the extent that he had, at the beginning, retained a wrong set of values, but who committed murder in uniform, added to theft and embezzlement, and in general behaved violently and hypocritically from the beginning. Yet this was never found offensive by anybody, at least not by anybody who wrote about it, and no audience I heard of raised any kind of protest after seeing it. And that was considerably earlier . . .

"It certainly is fantastic the degree to which the English class structure influences practically every Englishman's life, either in rebellion against it, or acceptance of it, or simply through their being gotten at by it without realising it, and sometimes whilst violently protesting that they're not." *Joseph Losey* (J.D.L.)

"We're all more or less blind; we can see precisely only the things we work with every day"; Jan van Rooyen's remark states the unifying theme of *Blind Date*, one of Losey's two finest and most complex movies to date. The vision of each character in the movie is limited by his experience, by the facts of his social existence. No-one can see clearly. This is true, even, of the audience viewing the film; the general rejection of the idea of Scotland Yard complicity in the covering-up of a sex scandal involving a diplomat was a manifestation of precisely the moral blind-spot which the film exposed. Critics coarsened the subtle truth the film embodied into a suggestion of "corruption" (thus evoking the "Corruption at Scotland Yard? Ridiculous idea!" reflex), an establishment response not unlike that of the representative in the movie of the establishment, Sir Brian Lewis, the Assistant Commissioner of Police, who says of his friend, the diplomat Sir Howard Fenton, who has been keeping the murdered Jacqueline Cousteau: "He can't possibly have any direct connection with this woman's death." Lewis knows; it's "A question of background." Thus it would not be in the public interest for Inspector Morgan to pursue a line of investigation which might involve Sir Howard. It might "upset important negotiations" which Sir Howard is carrying on for the British Government. It would be better to convict van Rooyen quickly, even if he is let off with a manslaughter charge which he may be persuaded to plead guilty to, than undertake a lengthy search for evidence. If Morgan is to go right to the top — he has the ability to do so — he must reveal "An understanding of the deeper

82

meanings of public service." Sir Brian is not attempting to tell Morgan what he must do ("It's your case, Morgan. The decision is entirely yours."); nor has he been in any way corrupted by outside forces. He is just stating the facts as he *sees* them: unnecessary scandal should be avoided, particularly if it is likely to harm the national interest. Losey convincingly evokes, through Morgan's prurient fascination with Jacqueline Cousteau, with her apartment, with her underwear, the kind of sexual infatuation which would make an important diplomat risk his self-respect and his career for a call-girl, and depicts with uncanny accuracy the kind of upper-class "old boy" solidarity which would help to conceal this liaison. Four years later, it was this lack of awareness, and this kind of desire to preserve the solidarity of the establishment, that enabled the Profumo affair to take on such far-reaching proportions. *Blind Date* comments on the moral awareness of a whole society, from the self-deceiving establishment down to the little postman who rounds vindictively on Jan when he guesses he is a suspect. Thus, Jan's jaunt through the sights of London evokes more than a real sense of place; it provides the social framework for the drama. Parliament Square, symbolic of the British tradition of democracy and public service, is symbolic, too, of the belief in the complete integrity of that tradition which is questioned by the movie.

If the vision of the members of the establishment is limited by their "background", that of Jan van Rooyen is similarly limited and that of Morgan almost distorted by their shared working-class backgrounds. Just as the thriller was the ideal vehicle for Losey's concerns in *Time Without Pity*, so the mystery is the ideal genre for the investigation Losey undertakes in *Blind Date*. The movie is essentially about the processes of deception and revelation, about 'seeing' and 'seeming', about illusion and reality. The progress of the film is a progress through illusion and deception towards reality and truth. The truth is something which is difficult to see precisely because deception and self-deception, the simple answers, present a less complex, less challenging, more comfortable picture of the world. Morgan, Jan, the audience participate in a search for truth; here, the convention of the mystery takes on a heightened significance; thus, knowledge of the plot would lessen the sense of confusion, and then the revelation, that a spectator experiences on seeing the film for the first time. The kind of fresh awareness one gains from seeing *Blind Date* corresponds very closely to the kind of fresh awareness both Jan and Morgan gain as a result of Morgan's investigation (Morgan's first action in the movie is to switch on the lights in the apartment in which Jan has been detained; he tells Jan: "I'm conducting an investigation . . . "). Morgan's search for truth — his refusal to accept an account such as Sir Brian's, which does not square with what he has been able to see of Jacqueline Cousteau: "She wasn't a giver. She was a taker" — can be read as a metaphor for the artist's search for truth; the relationship between Morgan and Jan is almost that of artist and audience, or analyst and patient, though Jan is not an audience, a non-contributing recipient of Morgan's vision of the world, but a stubborn, intractable obstacle which must somehow be incorporated into that vision if that vision is to be whole. Though Morgan is dissatisfied with Sir Brian's manslaughter deal, he tries it out on Jan, testing him. Jan replies that that would be to let the real murderer go free. At dawn, after an exhausting night of questioning, Jan starts to fight back, realising that he needs to search rather than merely state what he believes to be true if he is to escape from the trap that has closed round him: "Who sent her those cheques every week? Morgan, what are you hiding?"

Both men learn about themselves from the solution of the mystery. Despite his distaste for the "old boy" network as represented by Sir Brian Lewis, and for the self-deceptions Sir Brian represents, Morgan shares some of Sir Brian's illusions about society, and is thus for a long time unable to believe the truth he is starting to see: "I thought I had none of that left in me," he says when he realises how respect for the upper-classes has affected his judgment in the case. Morgan has been deeply affected by his class experiences. He is full of chip-on-the-shoulder remarks ("Friend of yours, sir?"), surface hostility, precisely because he feels he does not fit in with people like Sir Brian, or his own fellow Inspector, Westover; it is as if the latter's sarcastic remarks about his style of dress ("Been weekending in the country?") had really gotten through to him, making him feel inferior. He projects his own sense of social inferiority on to Jan: he refers to Jan's account of his affair with a society lady as "The sort of bragging lie kids like to tell," thus evoking a vision of upper-class life as seen by the lower-classes not dissimilar to that of Strindberg's Jean in *Miss Julie* (a very *Losey* character, both victim and exploiter, who has affinities with both Barrett and Webb Garwood). Morgan's consciousness is very closely related to that of a Jean, a Barrett, or a Garwood; it is his passion for truth, his ability to find meaning and significance outside his own selfish concerns that distinguishes him from them; he is not crippled as they are; he is someone who is able to learn, and to use his social experience creatively. When he tells Sir Brian that Jacqueline Cousteau "wasn't a giver. She was a taker", Sir Brian challenges him: "You sound as if you know?"; "I do. My father was a chauffeur"; this, too, is "A question of background." (In a beautifully subtle image later in the movie, Morgan and Jan are speaking to Jan's Jacqueline, Lady Fenton, when her chauffeur moves into the background of the image to say: "I have Sir Howard's luggage in the car, whenever you're ready, Lady Fenton". *Blind Date* is a movie of incredibly tight organisation —witness the motif of ice and fire running through it: "Ice can burn," 'Jacqueline' tells Jan early in the movie; face to face with Jan at the end, Lady Fenton goes to the fire to warm herself; the action, as well as having organic connection to the theme and symbols of the movie, is psychologically absolutely right at this moment).

There is some justice and accuracy in Morgan's description of Jan as a kid when placed in the environment of the affluent. Morgan questions Jan about the fact that his fingerprints were found all over the apartment; Jan admits his fascination with the apartment; he "wandered around looking at things"; "And washed your hands? Why, were they dirty?"; Jan admits sheepishly, "I just wanted to know what the soap smelt like." Morgan responds to the admission; Jan's behaviour is something he can understand. Though Jan is deeply intolerant of the world of appearances and deceptions that his Jacqueline comes from (like Morgan, he speaks as if he were confident that he has "none of that" left in him), the aggressiveness of his lectures also reveal him as being particularly vulnerable, frightened even, because inexperienced. He wants to reject his Jacqueline's feminity: "Women adore small meaningless attentions," she says, "like being helped with a coat"; when she suggests he teach her to paint, he challenges her motives: what does she really want? "To play a game?"; "Painting is work," he says, "Do you think you can paint until your head aches . . . ?" He does not want to have an affair with her: "If you want to play games, find somebody else." He is dominated by his background; his art is a masculine evocation of struggle and work, and therefore incomplete: he can state categorically: "The human body is a continent. You can spend a lifetime exploring it," but he flinches away when Jacqueline responds flirtatiously to the sexual implications of the statement. Yet those sexual implications are an essential part of the full import of the statement. Jacqueline is quick to notice that he does not paint women. Jan's need for a relationship in which he can grow, his need for sexual love, companionship and communication, make it possible for Jacqueline to ensnare him in the illusions and deceptions of her society, deceptions symbolised by the décor of the ostentatiously vulgar apartment in which he is detained; the education he undergoes during the course of the movie is essentially a process of liberating him from what that apartment represents. His relationship with Jacqueline makes him unable to see clearly: he tries to paint her, but cannot. He senses what is wrong, and turns to Jacqueline: "Have you ever given? Really given? Poured it out in a flood?"; she replies: "I don't know what you mean." He painted an old woman once, "ugly, worn, reptilian," and thought he had created something beautiful. Then, he produced something true, but now he is blinded by deceptions which are intimately connected with his idealism, an idealism which, because honest, is his strength, but which, because naïve, is his weakness. The flashbacks, illustrating Jan's account of the affair, are set in bright, well-lit places (art galleries, a studio); the apartment and the police station where Morgan interrogates Jan are lit so that they appear dark, oppressive. The truth seems something dark and evil, the deception clear and beautiful. Though the lighting of the flashbacks expresses Jan's idealisation of the affair, the action seems to be recorded objectively, an expression of Jan's essential honesty, an honesty which comes across, too, in the letter he sends to Jacqueline, and which Morgan reads. Morgan claims that letters like it frequently crop up in murder cases: "Not as well written as this, but the same general idea" — an insensitive remark, because the quality of the writing is an expression of Jan's whole personality, which is that of a creator not a killer: he writes "I haven't been able to work and that's where I get off." The lighting in the final sequences of the movie, though they are not in flashback, is less murky; the destruction of his illusions has made the truth more acceptable to Jan; the flash of illumination and revelation when Jan glimpses his Jacqueline again occurs in a brightly-lit exterior at London Airport. Jan does not cling desperately to his illusions, whereas, say, Tony in *The*

Servant has nothing else to cling to. Jan is an artist, and is therefore able to find meaning and significance outside his own personal concerns (though their vision may be limited, Losey's artists are creative in precisely the way that Antonioni's are not). He thus has the strength to face the truth and survive.

Jan's Jacqueline obeys the rules of the game: emotions are subordinated to appearances; a prisoner of her own society, she cannot avoid superficiality — in art, in love — and she is incapable of the self-discipline which goes with genuine freedom (she cannot see the point of the drawing exercise Jan sets her). Jan loves her and makes love to her with a passion and genuine emotion which touches her. It is something outside her normal experience. Jan allows himself to believe that a woman as superficial, as concerned with appearances, as Jacqueline could feel genuine emotion for him, that this is, for her, more than just a sexual adventure. And he becomes sufficiently involved in the relationship for his work (the symbol of his inner freedom) to suffer. This then is the illusion that Jan allows to be built up around his relationship — that superficial sexuality is in fact love. The apartment in which he is arrested symbolises this kind of sexuality. In fact it belongs not to his Jacqueline, but to the real Jacqueline Cousteau. It is cheaply vulgar, just as her underclothes are cheaply sexy, and she a cheap woman on the make. Jan's account of Jacqueline does not square with this picture at all (one of the facts that first arouses Inspector Morgan's suspicions) but objectively his Jacqueline is much closer to the real Jacqueline than she is to Jan, or to Jan's image of her. She is a product and a prisoner of the same kind of society: the society that values appearances above reality, teasing affairs above love, money above all. Although Jan's Jacqueline has a taste the real Jacqueline does not possess, this is more a sensitivity to fashion and convention than a genuine, felt sensibility. And she is in no sense the real Jacqueline's moral superior; both give themselves to men they want to make use of. The society which produces the one Jacqueline will inevitably produce the other. Except . . . except that Jan did arouse in his Jacqueline a spark of genuine emotion. It was not all pretence, Jan's vision of the relationship was not entirely self-deception. But this spark of emotion is her downfall; it forces her to recognise Jan at the police-station, and she has played the game too hard to be able to break the rules, even for a moment, without being destroyed. As Morgan says: "You're a woman a man remembers." The code is strict and allows no exceptions. Love, emotion, are breaches of the rules, and leave the individual in particular danger. Yet they are the standards by which those who are outside this emotional prison, and free from the constraints of the code, order their lives. Thus Jacqueline's final words to Jan — "Damn you" — have more than just a personal significance. They are the curse uttered by a society that has no place for the kind of sympathy, communication and strength that he represents: a curse on art, growth, creativity, on all that undermines the highly specialised adaptation necessary for survival in the world of the Jacquelines; the curse of negation. Growth, communication, sympathy, awareness of something outside oneself, give meaning to relationships, and thus, in an agnostic universe, to human existence. Life and creation are for Losey the process in which man fulfils his deepest spiritual needs.

13. The Criminal

"BANNION was modelled after someone that I know who is very active in the so-called underworld. And a man who, if his life had taken another direction, could have been a great executive, could have done anything he wanted to, because he has brains, he has humour, he has power, but he has been pushed into this criminal world from which there is really no escape once you get into it. And they have their own code, and their codes of loyalty and behaviour are absolute, and if you violate them, the penalties are much greater than in the outside world. But every once in a while this kind of man lets loose a physical kind of violence that is animal and insane and terrifying, and anti-social in a way that no society could tolerate, and I have seen this behaviour in the man that I know. And I can like him; I am interested by him, but I would always be frightened of him because underneath there is an animal that would do anything. And this is what I tried to present in Bannion, that this is waste, that the prison system hasn't changed, that it doesn't help, that it is a reflection of the society outside, that it has its own organisation, its own immediate parallels. It is at once more loyal, more sentimental, more violent, but it's the same thing, and one creates the other." *Joseph Losey* (P.v.B.)

The image of the prisoner, confined "within the limitations, inadequacies and degeneracy of his own desires"[7], is central to Losey's art — clarifying the attitude which one should take to the behaviour of characters in his earlier and subsequent films. It is a vision of one aspect of humanity not dissimilar to the psychologist Wilhelm Reich's account of *homo normalis*.

The Criminal opens with a succession of fourteen close-ups, of a *circle* of men gambling for thousands — calculating, bluffing — then the camera tracks back, placing the action in context: the men are prisoners, and they are gambling for, apparently, cigarettes. At the end of the film, two men *circle* Johnny Bannion's dead body, looking for the thousands in bank notes he has buried, whilst Suzanne, who throughout the movie has represented a freedom from

[7] Robin Wood in *Motion* No. 4 *op. cit.*

the mercenary concerns of Bannion's society, walks off at a tangent. Losey cuts back to the prison, and the end title flashes up; the image fades, then the final shot[8], background to the cast-list, fades in: a group of prisoners at exercise, shuffling round in a circle — "a comment on a society that has made money its god, and hence imprisoned itself in a vicious circle." (Robin Wood, *op. cit.)*

This possibly unconscious fusion of an image from Wordsworth ("Shades of the prison house . . ." — the theme is taken up again in *The Damned*) and one from Eliot's *The Waste Land* ("I see crowds of people, walking round in a ring") is the expression of one of the underlying tensions of Losey's art, the tension between a vision of society as a corrupting, deadening force, destroying individual creativity, and a vision of man's acceptance of a purposeless, sheep-like conformity, his individual responsibility for the meaninglessness of his existence. Losey combines a 19th century belief in the educability of man with a 20th century pessimism which results from man's inability to find fulfillment in a world in which traditional standards and values are decaying or collapsing. Even when his films lack a protagonist who is educable, their purpose is educative.

After the pre-credits card game, Losey cuts to the prison, then to Kelly, a prisoner returning; Kelly's return is shot in one long, fluid take (background to the credits: pressure of time seems to have meant that Losey was forced to use some of the film's key images as a background to either the beginning or end credits). Kelly's movements are circumscribed — he cannot walk out of frame. He is stripped of his personal possessions, given the uniform of the prison: in one shot, the routine of the prison is established, and the nature of the threat it represents to personal identity and freedom made clear. Kelly is being drawn back into the world of the prisoners,

---

[8] This extremely powerful shot was for some reason missing when *The Criminal* was shown during the 1966 Losey season at the National Film Theatre.

a world of which Scout, who carries messages around the prison, who has been there so long "he's forgotten they did away with the no-talking rule", is a symbol, heightened and extreme perhaps, but nevertheless representative. The camera zooms in on Kelly as a warden's hand comes down firmly on his shoulder, and, startled and nervous (he has betrayed the code of the prisoners, and is about to be punished for it), he is marched away to the cell-block.

The prison is, at one and the same time, a compelling general symbol for those who have given up the struggle to find purpose in life, retreating into a defensive shell, and, at the same time, a reproach to the society which allows it to exist. Its inadequacies symbolise society's lack of concern with essentials — the materialism that determines the lives of the prisoners dominates, too, the thinking of the society which incarcerates men in such an environment. Losey set out to reveal "the total inadequacy of the prison system" (G.O.O.); any kind of prison system is "an outrage and a self-perpetuating horror, but these medieval dungeons ... are something that most people just shut away from themselves" (G.O.O.). Their existence implies a judgment on the society that tolerates them.

The prison is presented as an autonomous society with rules of its own. The inmates (wardens and prisoners) are united by the fact that they are together *inside*: their relationship, their common complicity in violence (symbolised by the moment when Barrows, the chief warden, bangs his key on the railing, picking up the rhythm of the chant which the prisoners have set up as a background for the beating-up of Kelly — it is a near-sexual outburst which grants both Barrows and the prisoners *release*) is determined by their physical environment and the facts of their situation (a handful of hard men being set to guard and control several hundred hard men).

The power structure of the prison has evolved out of what the wardens and prisoners see as their needs; it has little relation to what the Governor or reformers in society at large believe it to be. Reform from the top is impossible; a change could only come in a radically different set of circumstances: new prisons containing fewer prisoners, and more (and more highly trained) wardens. But such a new prison could only be the product of a radically different society, one on the side of growth and life, whose code is not a grasping materialism and possessiveness which has its origins in human weakness and lack of identity. Thus the well-meaning reformist Governor — *New Statesman* reader, Fabian in approach — fails: he accepts the power-structure as it is, and attempts to work through it. He does not really understand the prison — at times he seems to want not to understand — and takes refuge in a kind of upper-class mateyness: "Skedaddle," he tells Scout when he wants him out of the way; "Stranger things have happened at sea," he says about the changes in Bannion's way of life that might result if he were to collaborate with the police. It is the only way left to him to express his sympathy with the prisoners. Losey wanted the character to convey more sense of an effort to break through, and would ideally have liked a warmer actor than Noel Willman to have been cast in the role. However, he uses Willman's qualities as an actor to convey a sense of resignation or abdication not uncommon amongst intellectuals of his class and generation: Willman's Governor knows he's beaten, and just goes through the motions of being a humanitarian.

The effective power in the prison, therefore, lies in the hands of three men: Barrows, whose power derives from his position of chief-warden; Frank Saffron — a calm, bland organisation man, more like a business executive than a criminal (a responsible head of a family, planning the purchase of a confirmation dress for a young girl in his family, his manner somehow suggests that he controls not so much an ordinary family as a tribal kinship network, a tightly-knit socio-economic unit from whose existence he derives much of his power and status in the underworld, his place in the organisation, and the contacts with the outside world from which springs his status inside the prison); and Johnny Bannion, a leader of men, loyal to his mates, warm, tough, acting impulsively and on his instincts. Each needs the co-operation of the other if their projects are to work smoothly, but each uses the other as far as he can. In this sinister world of secrecy and conspiracy, which baffles even Barrows ("I don't know why you or Saffron do anything, but I'm not having a killing in my prison. It would look bad on my record," he complains after Saffron has fixed it to appear that Bannion "let the screws in" to quell a riot, thus ensuring that Bannion is given a transfer out, and a chance to escape), a man such as Bannion is doomed ultimately to fail. The threat that Barrows represents is so obvious that it causes Bannion little real trouble; he easily "sees off" O'Hara and Flynn, whom Barrows hoped would beat Bannion up and thus give Barrows revenge for an insolent remark earlier in the movie. After doing so, Bannion looks up as Barrows enters the cell, with the defiantly gleeful expression of a small boy who is extremely pleased with what he has done. However, Bannion's refusal to see or accept the changes that are taking place in the structure of the underworld, changes which involve everyone except himself, makes him too trusting of Frank Saffron. There has ceased to be a place for an uncompromising individualist such as Johnny Bannion.

Bannion is certainly presented as admirable compared to those adapted to succeed in his society — Saffron, the smiling Mike Carter — but his limitations are nonetheless clear. He is intensely insecure, dependent on women: his voice betrays a fearful anxiety when Suzanne seems about to leave his apartment after their first encounter: "There's no hurry, is there?" After the robbery, he uses some of the money to buy her an expensive bracelet — a spontaneous, warm action, but one in which, characteristically, he expresses his love in materialistic terms. It is this action that leads to his re-arrest. When he is re-arrested he is unable to put an expression of their love into words; she has to. He never truly frees himself from the prison, as represented by its grandiose extension in the decor of his apartment. On his return to his apartment, he piles his clothes neatly on the table, according to prison ritual, then, realising what he has done, knocks them angrily to the floor. When, later, he escapes he desperately wrenches his handcuffs off. He is aware of the hollow nature of his fame; a young gangster asks admiringly about the fact that he was "big, inside," and Bannion replies bitterly about the harshness of prison life, the lack of privacy. He is tormented by guilt — his ex-girl friend Maggie gives an hysterical account of his reaction when a priest refuses to accept the candles he had purchased. When he is cornered by his past, he fights desperately to save himself and Suzanne — but he is forced to lead Carter to the field where he has buried the money as he needs it to get away to start a new life. As, dying from gunshot wounds, he staggers drunkenly out into the middle of the field, he has to gasp "Go away" to Suzanne, desperately making her leave him, as, if she does not, she will be murdered by Carter. Bannion must die without Suzanne, die in Carter's arms, not responding to Carter's questions about the whereabouts of the money, alone with his fears of hell and eternal damnation, surrounded by an expanse of snow, white and pure. Suzanne, dressed in white, but carrying Bannion's black coat, walks sadly away; Carter gives her a glance but, scrabbling like an insect in the snow, decides the search for the money is more important. Bannion is a Catholic, and believes in an afterlife, his vision of which is circumscribed by his experience in life: a sinner, he will be imprisoned in hell: "I dread the pains of hell!" he babbles desperately. Instead of bringing him release, freedom, religion extends his imprisonment beyond the grave. For Losey, religion is just another form of escape: whilst Saffron and Bannion plot during mass, Barrows undergoes an experience of near orgasmic intensity — a release of tension, but something whose effect is in no way permanent. After the death of Bannion, Losey wanted to cut back to Barrows banging his keys on the railing, thus stating explicitly a point which he was only allowed to imply: "in a sense he's still imprisoned there and he was part of the rhythm of the whole prison thing." (G.O.O.)

A few tiny incidents express the difference in attitude between Bannion and Mike Carter. On his release from prison, Bannion is met by Carter, who jokingly sets him a sum, which Bannion immediately does in his head. "Same old Johnny," says Carter; "Same old act of faith," replies Bannion, implying that Carter would accept any answer he gave. Carter replies that he had calculated the answer in advance. It is Bannion who makes the act of faith. After Maggie's hysterical outburst, Carter offers to deal with her. "Don't let that *thing* touch me," she screams, and Bannion tells Carter that there is to be no rough stuff. Later, a piano-tuner is quietly at work in Bannion's apartment when Bannion and Suzanne burst out of the bathroom, disturbing him, perhaps unintentionally shocking him, by their behaviour. He does, however, seem ultimately to respond to Suzanne's spontaneous joy; when Carter comes in, he purposefuly upsets the piano-tuner by striking a discordant note. Without healthy emotions, Carter can only establish his identity by setting out to provoke, antagonise; such actions are the only signs of the pressures that his apparently calm, unemotional adaptation involves. Lacking Bannion's individual personality, his strengths and weaknesses, Carter is perfectly suited to oust Bannion from the leadership of the gang, and work smoothly with "our mutual friend in Highgate." As crime becomes big business, using the techniques of big business, operators such as Bannion become inefficient. In the underworld, as in

THE DAMNED. Above,
Freya (Viveca Lindfors)
is shot down whilst
working on her sculpture.
Below, Joan (Shirley
Anne Field), watched
over by one of Bernard's
helicopters, heads out
to sea in Simon's boat,
where both will inevitably
die of radiation sickness.

EVE: Eve (Jeanne Moreau). "*The subtlest reactions of a character need to be mirrored in the face rather than expressed by sound and gesture.*"

normal business society, the growth of monopolies is driving out the Bannions; human possessiveness, in its desire for greater efficiency, is destroying Bannion's kind of individuality. Carter talks of the loot from the robbery as a "capital gain", speaking to the unknown figure in Highgate, whom he deferentially addresses as "Sir"; the robbery itself is staged at a race-track, at the Tote. Robbery, gambling, playing the stock-market: three ways, given luck, of making easy money, involving no true creative effort or responsibility towards society or humanity; all, therefore, purposeless and reprehensible.

14. The Damned

"I DON'T like violence, I don't like physical violence, but the world we live in is violent, and all of us are violent within ourselves, and I hope most of my films have interior violences of some sort. I don't like to show, I very seldom like to show actual physical violence in any kind of detail, and I always try to avoid the sensational." *Joseph Losey* (P.v.B.)

With the character of Bernard in *The Damned*, the image of the prisoner is extended to include those in the highest positions of political or bureaucratic power. Previously, characters who stand for life, growth, creation — Jan in *Blind Date*, the rather sketchy and unmotivated Suzanne in *The Criminal* (the character was forced on Losey, and he had little real opportunity to develop her part satisfactorily) — may have their safety endangered by their contact with the world of "the damned", the "prisoners", but they are not destroyed. In *The Damned*, not even the artist Freya survives. Political power such as that possessed by Bernard enables the "prisoners" to impose their degraded view of human existence on all mankind; with it, they are able to ensure that no one is left at large who has both the knowledge and the spiritual freedom necessary for effective action. Freya, Simon, Joan and King are all drawn inevitably into Bernard's project, and destroyed by their contact with it. There is no escape from the imprisonment Bernard represents. Not only is he, as a public servant, "the only servant who has secrets from his master", he is also the only servant who can impose his will on his master by exploiting his master's weakness, ignorance, apathy and fear. Bernard's project, born of death, could only be an act of public service in the time of a public indifference and abdication of responsibility so complete that it amounts to a rejection of life. Bernard's project, and his vision of the day of the megadeaths, are symptoms of society's (our) sickness, fear and evasion, and *The Damned* is a fable which diagnoses the spiritual malaise of modern humanity. In an important sense death (at least the moral death of escapism) is the end we and our society are seeking, and Bernard, the public servant, ministers to us just as Barrett, the manservant, ministers to his master. The concept of service underlying the Barrett-Tony relationship in *The Servant* (Barrett, the loyal servant, arranges for the gratification of Tony's unconscious desires) makes clearer some implications of *The Damned*; if Bernard, in one sense, corresponds to Barrett, *we*, society in general, must correspond to Tony. However, while Barrett's power is not sufficiently all-embracing to enable him to destroy Susan, Bernard's political power enables him to destroy Freya. Apparently Losey originally planned for her to be shot from one of the helicopters under Bernard's command, but his distributors insisted that a shot be inserted in which Bernard himself shoots her, so that the action should be "clarified". Nevertheless, the remote, depersonalised menace represented by the helicopters, symbols of Bernard's power, does come across very forcibly in the version of the film eventually shown.

Bernard, then, is the prisoner of a terrible vision of death, a vision of a universal nuclear catastrophe, and this makes his behaviour inhuman, although he *appears* to be a kind, reasonable and decent person. The defection of a man of Bernard's apparent qualities (he is Freya's friend, and seems to have been, perhaps even still to be her lover; presumably, therefore, he must once have been worthy of her love) emphasises how serious the situation is, and makes Bernard Losey's most frightening creation. Bernard is in command of a monstrous project; he is bringing up a group of radio-active children. These children have all been contaminated as a result of a nuclear accident during their mothers' pregnancies, and Bernard says that if he had sufficient knowledge to repeat such accidents at will, he would do so. He is educating the children to take over the world on the day the rest of humanity is destroyed in a nuclear war. He speaks of this with a passion that is almost love. The education he offers is, however, merely a form of imprisonment; indeed, he prefers to imprison minds by "education" than to resort to violence: he attempts to be less authoritarian in his approach to the children than the army officers with whom he works, whilst he argues with Freya before killing her, trying to convert her to his point of view. Her feelings and intellect tell her immediately that he is wrong, and she cannot willingly become a prisoner of his vision, but her deeply felt creative experience gives her a standard by which to judge Bernard. The children in the project have no comparable experience. Outwardly they are as much prisoners of Bernard's limited view of existence as is Bernard himself: they are uniformed; they speak very correct, precise English, and seem well disciplined and conformist. Bernard's teaching exemplifies most of what is wrong with modern "liberal" education. The children's studies consist of a potted introduction to Western culture, in addition to the science and technology necessary for their survival. Bernard is unable to accept the implications of the values he is trying to impart. He tries to *contain* the children's minds and imaginations. His education is the very opposite of a "drawing out", a road to intellectual growth, freedom and maturity. Remarkably the pupils recognise their prison (intellectual and physical) for what it is, and they rebel against it. In a scene of striking action and violence they destroy the television cameras and screens that link them with Bernard and the other controllers of the project. They rebel because they are imaginative and inquiring, and are unwilling to accept the limitations imposed upon them from above. "That isn't very democratic, Sir," Victoria, one of the girls, tells Bernard in an earlier scene when he refuses to answer a question. The philosophy of democracy has been put across in their education, but all their experience has been a denial of democratic practice. Perhaps if they had been told more about their situation the children would have been less likely to rebel, but Bernard withholds information from them because he considers they are too young to know the truth. He is protective: "I do not want the children to watch him die," he says when he discovers Simon has been in the children's quarters long enough to become contaminated by their radioactivity. But the children already have a conception of what death is. Moreover, there are certain questions which *must* be answered. The children must know why they are imprisoned, who and where their parents are. In the absence of informed answers to these questions they have invented their own mythological answers (some of which are fairly near to the truth). This mythology of course reflects the facts of their social existence. So, too, does their use of words. When Simon asks what something he has been given to eat *is* (what it is made of) he receives the answer "Lunch!" The children's terror of the "Black Death" (a soldier wearing black protective clothing who visits them nocturnally to inspect their dormitory, give them injections, etc.) reminds us of the dread that the figure of death himself inspired in the Middle Ages. They have good reason to fear the "Black Death"; he has removed from the dormitory children who were dying of radiation sickness; what is significant, however, is the superstitious nature of the terror he inspires: to the children he is a symbol of all that is unknown, and the truth could hardly have been more frightening than this supernatural figure. After the children's rebellion Bernard has to resort to force to recapture them. "The worst of this incident," he says, " is that my children will think of themselves as prisoners." But their first question to Simon, Joan and King is "Haven't you come to save us?" The children were hoping that they were their parents. Bernard has the power to confine them physically, even if he hasn't been able to control their minds, and no-one has the power to help them. Indeed, a few more years confinement may undermine their independence. "Someone help us!" the children cry from their rocky prison as the camera sweeps away across the landscape at the end of the film.

The character of Bernard shows, then, how the general will to destruction and self-destruction has taken over political power whilst maintaining a typically British appearance of respectability. The uniformed soldiers under his command, and King and his uniformed teddy boys, are the more obvious (and therefore less dangerous) manifestations of this violence. The identity of these two groups is clearly established: both wear uniforms and accept authoritarian discipline. The teddy boys march along the street whistling in Colonel Bogey style, whilst one of the army officers says at one point: "What that teddy boy needs is a good thrashing." "Black Leather Rock" (the theme song), with its refrain of "Smash! Smash! Smash! Kill! Kill! Kill!" applies equally to the two groups. (The violence of such pop-art is a reflection of the violence of the society that produces it; the song *exploits* these violent instincts, whereas Freya's sculptures, and Losey's movies, both quite violent, give expression to the pressures that underlie that violence.) Bernard comments, after Simon has been beaten up by the teddy boys, that the "age of senseless violence" has caught up with Britain, too, but he fails to realise that the all-embracing violence he represents is just as senseless, and infinitely more dangerous and destructive. Strong associations are established between Bernard and King. As King leads his gang in pursuit of Simon and Joan we see him in a graveyard, perched like a bird, on a tombstone, reminding us of the "graveyard bird" which is in Bernard's possession, and which is consistently associated with him. (This statue, Freya's vision of death, is given by her to Bernard at the beginning of the film.) Bernard's helicopters are birds of the modern age which bring violence and death. Bernard kills Freya, King tries to destroy her statues, which frighten him. King's violence is a function of his inarticulateness, his inability to communicate. He has no knowledge of sex, except a warped, strangely conservative fantasy: he describes Freya and others like her as "People with no morals." He has a perverted attachment to Joan — first trying to restrain her sexuality, then threatening, voyeur-like, to watch her and Simon's every move; Joan rounds on him: "You've never had a girl yourself." A moment later, though, he responds to her mothering. Freya struggles with him to protect her statues, and they roll to the very edge of a cliff. In Paul Mayersberg's words, "The destructive and creative desires of man, inspired by fear of annihilation and taking respectively the forms of instinctive violence and human protest, are locked together in a single embrace, and a common destiny."[9] The violence is born of fear, but its existence can only magnify this fear, not do anything to remove it. It is not a form of energy that can be usefully channelled. King does not grow or develop as a character. Although he helps Simon, Joan and the children against the guards, his violence here

[9] Paul Mayersberg writing on *The Damned* in *Movie* 9, May 1963.

is rooted in fear of the radiation sickness which has started to affect him. Physical sickness reinforces the instability of his emotional character, and his violent death is a fitting culmination to the violence of his life.

Simon, like many Losey characters (David Graham in *Time Without Pity;* Larry Wilder in *The Lawless,* who is — like Simon — played by Macdonald Carey) is an escapist. He has retired from the world of everyday life to sail the seas in his yacht "La Dolce Vita". He has actually adopted the carefree life many dream of. Although his version of "the sweet life" is very different from that of Fellini's characters, both involve the same kind of evasion of responsibility. However, the sea has brought Simon to Weymouth (where the action of *The Damned* occurs) just as later it is the route by which he, Joan and King reach Bernard's project. Although the sea *seems* to be a way of escape — for Simon from his mundane existence, for Joan from her brother King's incestuous jealousy — it in fact brings them to their destiny. One has a strong awareness of destiny in *The Damned,* as in *Eva.* It is not enough to say that in Losey's art character is destiny. This is only partly true. The existence of a destiny lying outside the psychology of the characters seems to be implied: in *Eva,* water brings Tyvian and Eva close together before a rainstorm actually brings about their first meeting. The peace that escape out to sea brings is beautiful in its tranquillity — the long-shot of Simon's boat lying motionless off-shore establishes this — but it is impermanent and illusory. As is so elsewhere in Losey's work, this kind of escape leads to death. When individuals abdicate their responsibilities, surrender their freedom of will, then their fate is determined by an external destiny. At the end of the film Simon and Joan, trying once more to escape, head out to sea, where they will inevitably die of radiation sickness.

Simon's escapism and abdication of responsibility are an essential feature of the kind of society in which Bernard and his project can flourish. Significantly, Simon is the character with whom the audience is most likely to identify. Simon is horrified by the project, and tries to rescue the children, but his new assumption of responsibility comes too late. He has discovered the project not through any act of volition, but by chance (or through the workings of destiny) and he does not know enough to take effective action until he and his companions are fatally contaminated by the radio-active children. What was reprehensible in Larry Wilder is, twelve years later, fatal in Simon. Simon, before he discovers the project, is involved with the sexually desirable Joan, but not with humanity.

Joan, like Simon, matures during the film, acting at one point as a mother-like protector to Simon, later to the children and even to King. Like Simon, she is educable — interested in finding out about people. She is the only true non-conformist of her group: when King leads his men in a motor-bike charge after her, gesturing like a cavalry officer, she turns right at a roundabout, taking the shortest route to the turning she wishes to take. King and his men very correctly go left, all the way round the roundabout. She condemns Simon for his attitude towards her; he deserved to be beaten up: "It takes two to play pretty little games ... You never even asked my name", but she wants something from him. There is a beautifully delicate moment when, after she has repulsed Simon, she does not move away from him: "I'm not holding you," he says, "you haven't moved." After they have made love she says, sadly, "I didn't want to be just somebody's girl"; Simon asks her to marry him; he has found a kind of peace with her: "It's as if I'm no longer afraid of dying." His relationship with Joan, though an escape, helps him to learn to *care* again. But, like Simon, Joan has chosen the illusory escape out to sea, and her assumption of human responsibilities comes too late to be of any

104

help to her or the other characters. Just as Simon has wasted too much of his time in evasion, Joan has wasted too much of her time in association with King and the violence he represents.

Only Freya lives a full, free, creative life. Significantly, she is the only character whose death has to be *willed*. An artist, named after the goddess who supplied the golden apples of eternal youth to the Nordic pantheon, she manifests a life force that could never be indifferent or escapist, a life force which is the human equivalent to the elemental beauty of the sea, and of the cliffs on which her workshop is sited: this is one of the few beautiful landscapes Losey has ever filmed; it has a kind of beauty which man seldom really understands or responds to; man's customary indifference is better reflected by the barren "waste lands" in which Losey usually photographs him. Only by the destruction of all that Freya stands for and is associated with can Bernard's project survive. She must be destroyed by the logic of his world. Even when she knows all Bernard's reasons for taking on the responsibility of the project, she cannot agree to keep its existence secret. She has told him, early in the movie, "I hate your secrets." She has witnessed the horrible scene when extra forces of guards and soldiers overpower and recapture the escaping children, and she is only willing to comprehend the project's cruelty. We, the audience, are also only able to judge Bernard on his actions, and their effects, not on his motives, for we have seen what freedom means to all the children — they blink at the sun like the Prisoners in *Fidelio*, one little girl runs happily to pick a flower — and we have shared the amazement of Henry (a little boy who, having developed a pathetic attachment to King, flees with him in Freya's sports car) when he discovers the wondrous size and beauty of the outside world: "It goes so fast, King. The world's so big." If Simon and Joan, through past indifference, complement the world of Bernard and King, Freya is its negation. It is *her* judgment of Bernard that matters, rather than Simon's outburst: "You're the man who knows all about violence! You're the man who knows all the answers." Her final action is typical: to carry on with her work until the last moment of her life. She has not wasted her time, or sought escape, nor does she when faced with death. The moral judgement which the film forces us to take against Bernard and in Freya's favour makes *The Damned* one of Losey's most radical films.

15. Eve

"YOU can't imagine what it is to see this film because, when I saw the Hakim version, I thought: 'How could I possibly have made a film that, even no matter what they did to it, was so bad.' But I like this. Most of it. But it is . . . very subjective. It would be a little better if I hadn't been so involved in it." *Joseph Losey* (P.v.B.)

"I think *Eve* was bound to be flawed for a variety of reasons. In the first place, I started from a book which I don't believe I ever was able to even read completely, but, as with film projects in my experience, you have a mixture of commercial and artistic considerations — with those very rare exceptions we all know about, like, notably, Bergman, and a very few others — and you've got to start somewhere, or you don't start at all. In this particular instance the Hakims owned this book which they wanted to make, and on which they'd spent a great deal of money for various scripts which I never even saw, and they also had made contracts already with Jeanne Moreau, whom I was very much interested in working with, or thought I was, and the thought was confirmed as soon as I met her. And they'd also already signed Stanley Baker, with whom I had worked with great pleasure on several previous occasions, so that was the beginning point, and I informed them clearly at the beginning that

106

I thought that various themes I wanted to explore could be explored through the book, and that I thought the general structure of it could probably be followed, although basically, from what I'd read of it, it seemed to me a very false book, and one obviously written for Hollywood consumption.

"So the first flaw, I think, is in the original material, to which one had to conform to some extent. This became more and more clear, and the final belated clarity came when one saw what the Hakims attempted to do to the film when it fell completely into their hands, partly through our stupidity and gullibility, because I think, had we been tougher at certain points, we could have kept control of the picture. We couldn't entirely control its making, but we could have kept control of it to a larger extent. To some extent, anyway. But what they expected, obviously, from me, I suppose because of *Blind Date*, *The Criminal*, *The Prowler* and others, was melodrama and sensation, and what they expected from Jeanne Moreau, because of *The Lovers*, was sex and sensation, and what they expected from Stanley Baker was violence, and they didn't really get any of those elements, at least not in the way they expected to get them, so there was, from the beginning, a cross-purpose of intention, though our intentions — by 'our', I mean mine, in particular, and Jeanne Moreau's in particular, and Stanley Baker's to a lesser degree — were very carefully defined to them, even to the point of initialling every page of the script that was written, before we shot. So that's one reason. The other reason was that there was such incredible circuitous intervention and obstruction, and lack of not only sympathy, but total lack of understanding of what we were trying to get at.

"My instinctive reaction, and I think that of many other people in my situation, but perhaps I do it more than others, is that once you feel the enmity of the people you have to deal with, the enmity to your idea, or to you, or to whatever it may be, even

107

though they've hired you, you go out of your way to protect ideas which, if left alone, you probably would reject. In other words, one has an idea about a particular characterisation; or even how to write a particular scene, and given a few days or a few weeks to think it over, or think twice about it, or even overnight if you've shot half of it, you may abandon the approach and do something else, but if somebody is saying 'You can't do it. You mustn't do it. It's wrong. It has to come out. You won't get the location, and I'll see to it that you won't get the location, I'll see to it that you don't get what you need to shoot it,' then, if you're at all obstinate in the preservation of your work and yourself, you go overboard to insist on it. Then when you look at it a year or two, or even a month, later, you think 'Oh, Christ, why did I do that?' and you know you did it because you felt that if you didn't protect it to this extent, it would be the opening wedge, and a lot of other things would fall to pieces. That's another reason why *Eve* is flawed.

"I think the picture that was finished, even the picture that was finished with a score of existing recordings of Miles Davis and Billie Holiday, to which I shot, and which I put on the work print for my own guidance, and for the composer's guidance, was by far the best film I have ever made and I think it would probably have stood up as a fairly considerable film among the few important films that have been made since the history of sound films. But that film was never seen, except by a handful of people who worked on it. And the finished one, with the new score and soundtrack on it, our own score and soundtrack, was in fact, not even seen by the people who worked on it, except in pieces. Outside of Gianni Di Venanzo, now unhappily and tragically dead, and one journalist friend of mine, nobody else ever saw it at all. But the Hakims of course did. So, there has been nothing shown for people to judge.

"There were and are various versions. The one that was shown in Paris had already had huge sequence cuts made. There were no cuts made *within* sequences in that version, but two or three key sequences had been removed. I'd already compromised the picture in an attempt to reach some sort of agreement with the Hakims, in good faith, which they didn't respect — by eliminating a great deal from the picture, in a re-cut version, that I think should have been in it. A great number of sequences which were essential to the original conception were never shot, because it was made impossible for me to get locations, and other things of this sort, and one or two scenes were shot under conditions that were so poor and so bad that I myself didn't include them because they didn't work, although I think they would have worked. That was another version, then. First of all, there was the work-print with the work-score, which I think was the best. Then there was the version that I finished, and that was the next best. Then there was the version that I re-cut for them, which I think was the next best. None of these were seen publicly, ever, by anybody. And next there was the version shown in Paris, which had sequences cut from it, but an unmutilated score and soundtrack and dubbing, and no cuts within sequences. Then there was the version which they made, of which there were various versions, in which they re-dubbed a number of the principal actors, destroying completely any conception of language unity — consistency of accents and the languages themselves — and in which they re-dubbed Virna Lisi to make her performance quite idiotic. In my version Anna Proclemer's dubbing of her was a great performance and along with Virna Lisi's very great beauty and expressiveness, I would have thought it a considerable performance. They re-dubbed Albertazzi, who is a great actor, and made his peformance quite ridiculous, apart from cutting out the key parts of his sequences. They added words of their own which were banal and vulgar, off-screen and in asides, they took out lines that were key. They added certain lines, re-dubbed certain lines of Moreau's and added certain lines off-screen of Moreau's, with another voice imitating hers. They eliminated what I consider to be one of the great soundtracks of all time, which we spent months making; they didn't eliminate it altogether, but they changed it around without any sense of the rhythm of the picture, the intention, or the poetic qualities in it, which were necessary against the harshness of the subject and the cruelty of some of the treatment. They messed about with a really marvellous score. I have some reservations about the score, but on the whole I think it's quite a brilliant score, and it was intended as a whole piece. This they juggled with, changing the position of pieces of music, fading music in and out, taking it out entirely in certain places, inserting it in places where it didn't belong, and adding other bits of music that were just idiotic where they came. In other words, it was a complete piece of destruction. The one thing, in all of the versions, that was never mine, and that I was never able to win any kind of battle about, was the titles, which were very carefully conceived as title backgrounds, and were fairly essential both to the style and the meaning of the picture. And this they interfered with from the beginning, and put their own typography on, and also put it in the wrong places, so that right at the very beginning something that was an essential rhythm was destroyed.

"So, for all these reasons, it's flawed. It's also flawed because I was over-personal. I was probably over-attached to some aspects of Moreau's art, and perhaps made too much use of certain personal things that I found in Stanley Baker, instead of standing outside it a bit. I think the picture is slightly over-subjective and over-personal, and overpassionate. I don't think these things would necessarily have been faults in the long run. Anyway, that's quite a handful of reasons as to why it's flawed. I suppose it's the most tragic thing to say,

110

but I tried and tried again to get a copy of the original and I saw it on this occasion with Di Venanzo and a journalist, on a Sunday or Saturday morning in Rome, and the Hakims were not there. They'd made an appointment with me to view this compromise version which I had agreed, and I went to Rome, and they were not there, and through Di Venanzo I discovered that there was a print, and we saw the print, and I think came out of the theatre at about 1.30, and suddenly having full realisation of what I was up against in terms of complete breach of every agreement and every act of good faith I asked Di Venanzo to get the print out of the lab, and so he tried. But it had been removed almost at once by the Hakims, and it's never been seen again, and I don't suppose it exists any more, and I don't suppose the negative exists. But there were two or three copies of this print made, and I discovered, quite by accident, as you know, about two years ago, that one of these, in their attempt to save a little money, was sent to Holland for distribution. They probably figured this was an unimportant territory, and they didn't care, and anyway it would be subtitled, and this was in turn sold to certain Scandinavian distributors. Now by the sheerest accident, I was in Scandinavia on a reconnaissance trip for a new film I didn't make, and I learned that the people that we were dealing with had had enormous success with *Eve*, and I made my usual comment about it's not being mine, and they said that they were sure it was. I asked how long it was, and they said two hours and twenty minutes, which was the length of the second version — the original version was two hours and thirty-five minutes — and I asked if I could see it. It was covered with Scandinavian sub-titles (I'm deliberately being slightly vague about which country, as I don't think it's fair to the people concerned, though it's probably no secret), but, in any event, it was that version, entirely complete, excepting for a few frame-cuts that had obviously been made from a great deal of

111

running, and it was a pretty scratched up print, but still, it was a Di Venanzo print, which meant that it was highly superior, as among other things the Hakims watered down the print. Anyway, I asked if I could buy it, and since these people owned the print, they were only too glad to sell it. However, it was not within my means to pay out a very large sum of money for a print, just for private showing, no matter how much I wished it to be preserved, and it took me nearly a year to get the money from subsidy sources to buy it, and it was bought, but when it arrived it was nearly twenty minutes shorter. I immediately protested to the sellers, and they agreed that certain scenes that I'd pointed out were missing, and that they hadn't been missing before, and that the length was this much reduced, and that they would attempt to rectify it, and didn't understand how it could have happened. Then, some months later, a letter came saying that there had been no changes, and that they could do nothing about it, and that it was just as I had seen it, which is not true, and admittedly not true in their own correspondence.

"However, my only guess is that it took so long to finance the purchase that they put it out for distribution. Probably they were worried about the length, and made cuts for reasons of length. And they might very well, and quite understandably, have thought that I was never going to get around to arranging the purchase. So that accounts for these particular deletions. However, the cuts that were made in it were made skilfully, at least, whereas the others were cut abominably, and it does contain at least two sequences which are not in any Hakim version, and what there is of the soundtrack — I think it's just under two hours — is mine. So there are remnants of the original left. But that's the only thing that's preserved in any way, or ever will be, I should guess, unless there is negative stored away somewhere that somebody sometime,

EVE. Eve's *"determination to maintain some kind of independence in a world that's not a woman's world."* Tyvian (Stanley Baker), Eve (Jeanne Moreau) and the Greek (Alex Revides) at top. Centre: Eve with Francesca (Virna Lisi), her natural enemy. Below: the wedding, Francesca and Tyvian. Francesca insists on being married in her church, della Salute. *"Très chic. Très cher,"* comments Eve, *"Did she pay for it?"*

THE SERVANT:
The pervasive visual
motif of the film
is the triangle:
Vera (Sarah Miles),
Barrett (Dirk
Bogarde) and Tony
(James Fox).

some historian, may dig up. I should doubt it. I don't expect I'll be around."*

"The motivation of Eve is one of the things that suffered most."

"Eve wasn't written, in the book, and she wasn't written in the screenplay, in the sense of dialogue, and I attempted to explain Eve, not in words, but in images and in actions, and in different aspects of her life. The whole thing was very much tied up with the sound and sense of Billie Holiday, and Billie Holiday's autobiography, which Eve reads, and the kind of public front which Eve presented to various men, and the kind of private façade which she had when she was alone with herself, or alone with her maid. For instance, one of those sequences which was shot but never used — because I wasn't allowed to do it the way I wanted to, and it didn't work— was the scene of her confession, in church, in a church in Rome. Another one was a scene in which she's confronted by a racketeering pimp, who objects to the fact that she is a prostitute, essentially, but not working within their syndicate or within any kind of organisation. Another scene that was lost was a scene in which the syndicate attempts to intimidate her by having her mocked and pursued by a gang of teenage ruffians on the street. She finally ends in a hysterical flight from these kids, falling into an antique shop for protection, and being beaten up by them. All these things, obviously, were fairly essential to the picture, but they're not there, and never were there. They weren't even in the original version because I just wasn't able to shoot them. There's one particular location, for instance, in the picture, when she and Tyvian are out courting, she falls on the stairs, and suddenly finds herself up against a grimy old decayed street beggar. The Hakims didn't want the confrontation with the old woman and were so against this scene that the location I finally had to use for it was my *ninth* choice. They made it impossible for me to get

* See special note on National Film Archive print of *Eve* at end of chapter.

113

every other location that I chose. These were the obstacles of shooting. There was a time at which Moreau, the writer, the composer, Stanley Baker and I, and I think the art director and editor, drew up an injunction to restrain the Hakims from making any use of the picture — this was before it was finished, because they were already showing it in their own version. We learned then that they were selling it, falsely, they were selling it in their own version, not mine, privately, to distributors, and we drew up an injunction to restrain them, and under the copyright laws of Italy and France, particularly Italy, copyright belongs in perpetuity to the director, the composer and the writer, jointly. If we'd gone through with that injunction, even if the picture had stopped I believe it could have been re-financed and finished properly, and I think we should have done it. I must say that Moreau was extraordinarily courageous, and said to me: 'Do exactly what you want to. It's your decision. You do it. Whatever you decide to do, we'll stand behind you.' But her agent, among other people, put great pressure on me, and said: 'How can you take the responsibility for this? If the shooting is stopped at this point, you may never re-finance it, it may never be taken up again, the actors may not be available when you get around to finishing it, and it's better to go on and finish it, and not run this risk,' and so I decided to abandon the injunction, which I think we should never have done . . .

"I think the important thing about Eve is that she never attempted to explain herself, and the most explanatory thing, I think, was her defence of her privacy, and her last words to him were that she'll meet him, *if* she comes back: in other words, the determination to maintain some kind of independence in a world that's not a woman's world, and where women are the extremes of various things — such as Eve's particular extreme — because of what's demanded of them by men. It's interactive, and there are extremes in men, as in Tyvian, because of the way they treat women,

114

because of the way they use women, and because, again and again and again, human life, from childhood, early childhood up, is distorted by the insistence on conformity and the attempt to conform to codes and ways of life that hardly any thinking adult believes in. We live in a society which intellectually and scientifically and humanly and emotionally rejects all kinds of really totally outmoded forms, and, at the same time, is shocked by anybody who doesn't live by them; and people continue to live by them themselves to the point where they either go mad, or are blunted and corrupted and brutalised. Some few individuals find their own protection against vulnerability and their own means of survival, by simply making their own rather air-tight, logic-tight little cell to live in. That's what Eve did, and that was what Tyvian tried to do but failed to do ... It upset people because most people either don't make the fight, or make it abortively. As Mosley said in *Accident*, people go in occasional jumps and starts, sudden jumps and starts, but otherwise most people's lives are devoted to what is called killing time, you know, getting by, getting through another day, getting through another night, whether it's the agony of Tennessee Williams, or whether it's the obliviousness of habitual gamblers, whatever it may be." *Joseph Losey* (J.D.L.)

"Losey creates many of his effects by keeping his eye on brand names. Yet in *Eve* his eye appears to have been a little blurred. Billie Holiday records may be in character, but no contemporary courtesan worth her salt would risk her reputation on reading something so old hat as the *Poesie di T. S. Eliot*. Robert Lowell perhaps, but Eliot ... ?" *Eric Rhode*[10]

"Mr. Losey tells me that Jeanne Moreau as Eve at no time reads *Le Poesie di T. S. Eliot*. Apparently the book belongs to the hero's fiancée who is old-fashioned, 'Even by Italian standards'. My apologies then to Mr. Losey and to all contemporary courtesans

[10] Eric Rhode: *The Day of the Butterfly*, Sight and Sound, Winter 1963-64.

worth their salt." *Eric Rhode*[11]
  "An Englishman, A witty Englishman?" *Tyvian Jones*[12]

Eve, perhaps Losey's most personal and subjective film, is, for
me, one of the very great films, and arguably Losey's finest work
so far. Despite all the mutilations in the Hakim version, and the
enormous barriers the Hakims raise to a full and intense appreciation of the film (the soundtrack is savaged, the re-dubbing is
crude, and does, as Losey says, make the performances of Virna
Lisi, and particularly Giorgio Albertazzi, ludicrous), I find even
their version a very great, if seriously imperfect work of art. Once
one has started to respond to the formal pattern of the work, and
to its central pre-occupations, the surface defects of the Hakim
version start to matter less: at a deeper level, the Albertazzi character is in no way ludicrous. However, for Losey these defects
cripple the film: he is a modest man, but he is a highly perceptive
critic of what is good and bad in his work, and he knows that the
soundtrack he and his associates created for *Eve* was a great
soundtrack; he feels that the film he made, despite a few technical
imperfections (he is, as has been indicated, a perfectionist) was an
excellent piece of craftsmanship: it worked on every level, including the surface level. Losey has every right to be bitter; it is
one of the great tragedies of film history that one should be forced
to overcome, for example, the barriers of apparently ludicrous
acting performances before one can respond to one of the most
profound and beautiful works of the cinema. It is also tragic that
the essential poetic rhythms of the film — an integral part of Losey's
conception and purpose — should have been destroyed: there *is*
poetry, very intense poetry, in the Hakim *Eve*, but the fragments

[11] Eric Rhode: letter published in *Sight and Sound*, Spring 1964.
[12] Tyvian during a squabble with two Englishmen in the hotel bar, shortly before
his "confession" scene.

116

that remain of the Losey *Eve* — preserved in the print at the National Film Archive — give one a glimpse of the beauties and richness that the Hakims have denied us.

Eve opens and closes with the statue of Adam and Eve standing by the tree of life. The story is largely told in one long flashback, when the appearance of Branco Malloni in a bar where Tyvian Jones, a writer turned guide, is entertaining a group of tourists forces back into Tyvian's memory the story of his relationship with Eve and with his wife, Francesca, the anniversary of whose death it is. The misery enacted between the opening and closing shots is an indication of the destructiveness of emotional relationships in which there is no true organic link. Thus the film is not the near-documentary study of prostitution that a critic such as Mr. Rhode tries to make of it, and the naturalistic criteria Mr. Rhode applies to it are totally irrelevant. The story is acted out with Venice, which Tyvian describes as his Babylon, in the background. As always in Losey's films, décor and location are a symbol of as well as a setting for human actions and motivations. Though the churches of Venice may remind one of the stable moral traditions of the past, the city itself (once a trading port, now a tourist centre) is a symbol of past and present decadence and venality: Venice is one of the most luxuriant growths that have sprung from human affluence. It resembles a web in which the characters, Tyvian, Eve, Branco, Francesca, are enmeshed, and to which they continually return, unable to free themselves. Losey uses water — the sea, the canals, rain — very beautifully to suggest a destiny lying outside the characters: water carries Eve and Tyvian close to each other on several occasions (for example, when he is water-skiing, she passing in a boat) before eventually a boat-trip, a broken engine and a rain storm combine to bring about their first meeting. Though a destiny which lies outside human volition plays a part in the story, what happens is essentially a product of the behaviour of the characters,

117

and the psychological, moral and social factors that underlie their behaviour. The film is centrally about the relationship between man and woman in a society dominated by traditions which no longer have a living, vital creative force, and which are therefore more likely to inspire shame and destructive guilt than health or growth. Tyvian and Eve are cut off from the sustaining power of traditional religion (this is implied by the shot of the church seen through the key-hole), but they have not emancipated themselves from the repressive moral code of Christianity. Tyvian's claim "I stopped worrying about church and chapel a long time ago" is just one of his many self-deceptions. His background dominates his behaviour throughout the movie. His aggressive Don Juanism is an expression of his inability to sustain a deep relationship, and this is, in turn, connected with his shame; his attraction to Eve stems partially from the same source. She is so attractive sexually precisely because she is a whore, selling her body to the rich: a concise image of the emotions imposed on the male by a repressive society. His confusion at seeing McCormick when in Eve's company is symptomatic of his attitude. McCormick's comment after Tyvian has left — "That costs money" — pinpoints another aspect of Eve's attractiveness: to possess Eve, even for a night, signifies that one has made it in the materialistic society the film depicts. Moreover, Eve is selective; she chooses whom she will sell herself to. If Tyvian represents an extreme of what guilt has done to men, Eve represents an extreme of what men do and have done to women: a synthesis and extension of the two Jacquelines in *Blind Date*. What she wants and needs is the husband she invents: "He's a real man. He can handle me." When she first meets Tyvian, she described this "husband" to him, as if making a plea "You be like that!" But Tyvian is not a man with a purpose in life, the kind of man who builds dams in Africa; he is a "loser". He has won fame with a novel about his experiences down the pit

118

back home in Wales, the film of which has made him rich, but he is unable to fulfil his contract with the film-maker Branco Malloni to produce a second book. Though his wife Francesca suspects what is wrong, he is able to confess only to Eve that not he but his dead brother wrote the novel. He talks about his brother's pride in his work, his strength and simplicity: "I'm only a working man"; about his brother's entrusting the novel to him: "See what you can do with it, Tyvian boy"; "And he loved me ... And I put my name on it. I stole my dead brother's soul." He begs Eve: "Help me," and lays his head childlike on her breast: *Eve* is the story of Cain and Abel as much as that of Adam and Eve: Losey has already told us, through the song written for the movie, "There was no Adam, there was no Eve": guilt is ever-present in human relationships. Tyvian confesses and seeks absolution from Eve, something which she cannot give. (She, too, was forced into a confession in the film Losey set out to make.) All she can do, faced with a need so similar to her own, is to encourage Tyvian to do what she has done, build a protective shell that cannot be penetrated, forget the guilt that is crippling him: "Does he need his soul?" she asks of the dead brother who is between them. The camera pans away from Tyvian up her horizontal body (they are lying on the floor of their hotel room) to frame her face — an expressionless mask which almost conceals her hopeless resignation: the shot defines a certain kind of cinema, one which derives from Strindberg's description of naturalism, of "the modern psychological drama" in which "the subtlest reactions of a character need to be mirrored in the face rather than expressed by sound and gesture." (Preface to *Miss Julie*).

Given the vulnerability of Tyvian and Eve, love is not possible: the shell that effectively disguises Eve's needs, the shell that Tyvian has been partially successful in adopting, forces them into a conflict in which Eve, the harder and more completely adapted, is inevitably the stronger. Their first meeting establishes the tone of their whole relationship. Francesca has left Tyvian to go on a business trip to Rome; Eve has arrived at Tyvian's island villa with a client whom she treats almost like a servant, as if demonstrating that, though he has paid well for the weekend, he does not own her. They are seeking refuge from a rainstorm; the motor-launch the client had hired for the weekend has broken down (the client, in turn, expresses his aggression against the crew of the boat). Tyvian terrorises the client into leaving: they are on his property, and he wishes to exercise his rights as a proprietor, and demonstrate his virility (this synthesis of the insights of both Freud and Marx in the treatment of sexual relationships is characteristic of Losey's work). Tyvian attempts to give expression to his feudal conception of sex by right of conquest, to find out what Eve can do: the camera looks down on them as they writhe on the bed (the shot is a summary, in advance, of their whole relationship), then Eve knocks Tyvian cold with an ornament. Later, they do sleep together. Tyvian boasts in advance of his virility: "I like to make women happy." Eve replies: "Let's see what you can do," and warns, "Don't fall in love with me." After they have made love, there is a shot of Tyvian, underlining his almost hysterical assertion of his masculinity: he says with satisfaction: "Not conceited, just accurate." Though up till then Eve has toyed with him, asking him if he has enough money to go to bed with her (one of her masks: the mask is the central visual motif of the sequence in which she asks this question, and a recurring motif, visual and psychological, of their relationship), leading him on into believing that they are going to sleep together, then slamming the door of her room in his face, she has, too, revealed her basic needs, telling him of her "husband", and hinting at her fear of the future. Tyvian has asked what she likes best in the world, and she replies: "Money"; "Why money?" he asks;

"To buy records," she replies: she is obsessed with the tragic (but creative) figure of Billie Holiday, whose anguish is her anguish; she takes her gramophone everywhere with her to play Billie Holiday records; she invents incidents from her past reminiscent of the life of the singer, a story of childhood seduction: "I was eleven, you understand," then adds teasingly, when Tyvian seems to believe her: "You'd believe anything." When Tyvian asks her what she hates most in the world apart from men, she replies "Apart from men . . . old women." They make love for the first time on the night she encounters the old beggar woman sleeping in the street — an experience which shatters her shell momentarily — it is as if she were turning to Tyvian for support. Before they make love, she confesses: "I think I'm ugly." Tyvian, in turn, has already told her about his chapel background — "You just can't forget it" — and admitted "I was never really a miner."

Eve, from the outset of her relationship with Tyvian, is in conflict with the respectable, virtuous Francesca, her natural rival: she sees Francesca's picture, finds her night-dress, sniffs it to see what perfume Francesca uses, and discovers a shelf full of copies of Tyvian's book *Stranger in Hell* (almost a parody of a Losey title), with Tyvian's picture on it, during her first few moments in his villa. When he first tries to "make" her, she is aware, therefore, of Francesca's recent presence. After they have eventually made love at Eve's, Tyvian returns to his town apartment. Francesca, who has come back early to surprise him, is asleep, clutching a translation of Eliot, a poet who, like Francesca, has sought help in a world of crumbling moral values in the traditional religious sanctions of the past (Francesca insists on being married in her church, *della Salute*), and who, unlike her, has found it. Tyvian tries to justify his behaviour to her in terms of his façade of virility: he says that he loves all women, six to sixty, and Francesca replies "And they're all the same, aren't they?" When they make

121

love, she says: "But with love, Tyvian. With love. *Con amore.*"
— comment enough on his virility. Immediately afterwards Branco
Malloni, who is in love with Francesca, comes by, bitter at the
fact that Tyvian has been seen in public with Eve. Tyvian responds
sarcastically, and with some justification: "It's all right, then, if
I'm discreet?" Though Branco seems to have a genuine affection
for Francesca — when he thinks that she is happy with Tyvian, he
ceases to press his campaign against Tyvian — he is a representative of a society that lives by a hypocritically strict code, a society
in which men both use and reject a woman such as Eve, a society
for which a sexual relationship between a guilt-laden Don Juan
and a call-girl is a valid, if heightened symbol, pointing to an
essential truth. Tyvian's initial willingness to flout the conventions
of this society links him to Eve, but he has neither the money nor
the strength of personality to go through with it. Eve ultimately
humiliates Tyvian through his relationship with this society: she
calls him up just as he and Francesca are due to go to the wedding
of Anna Maria and McCormick; he has begged her to spend a
weekend with him, and she says it must be this weekend, and no
other. He goes; after the scene of his confession, she demands
payment from him, then tells him it is not enough, but she doesn't
mind, as she has made new business contacts. She throws him out,
telling him to take his money: "You're a loser. Go on, loser. Take
it. You need it more than I do. You've earned it. Take it!" Tyvian
almost does so, but leaves taking only his cuff-links, watch and
cigarette-case, which he had offered as part payment. Eve is left
alone with the money, money which symbolises their joint failure
in the relationship. Earlier in the weekend, Tyvian had asked her:
"Do you know how much this weekend is going to cost me?", to
which Eve replied: "That's something my husband would never do.
Discuss money." Losey's camera lingers on Eve (as it does on other
occasions when she drives Tyvian away) as she wanders, tense and

pensive, though superficially calm, to the window, and stands smoking a cigarette, looking out over the city.

Eve responds bitterly to Tyvian's marriage to Francesca, his attempt to return to social respectability; she telephones him to ask why she was not invited to the wedding: "*Très chic. Très cher.* Did she pay for it? Have you told her about your brother?" She says she has sent Tyvian his money back: "I don't want your dirty money. *Pauvre tarte.*" Francesca partly overhears the call, and tells Tyvian: "I love you, Tyvian, but how can we ever make it work if you won't tell me. You must tell me." He replies: "I will. Don't go to Rome tomorrow". She says, as if to punish him for not confiding in her: "I think I will now." On two occasions when Tyvian expresses his need for her (here, and very early in the movie, earlier in the evening of Tyvian's first meeting with Eve), Francesca rejects him to go on a business trip, though normally she gives him support, and seems to understand him. Tyvian comments ironically to Eve at one point "Francesca, she believes in me," but Francesca withdraws her help at two crucial moments; what happens in the relationship between Tyvian and Francesca provides a parallel, on a less intense level, to what happens between Tyvian and Eve. When Francesca returns from her second trip, she finds Tyvian has been forced to sleep on the floor of the villa, whilst Eve has taken his bed, an act of revenge for Tyvian's behaviour: he has humiliated her in a night-club, and, later, struck her: "Only my husband can do that." Francesca runs desperately from the house to the motor-boat which brought her; then kills herself, crashing it head on into a wall across the water from the island. Just as Tyvian is too weak to handle Eve, Francesca is too weak to handle Tyvian. After Francesca's death, Tyvian's guilt and self-hatred force him to consider strangling Eve, but his obsession for her is so strong that he cannot even attempt to do so, and she drives him off with a whip (a present from one of her clients), crying "loser"

123

hysterically as she hits him. This terrible outburst of violence is the climax of the movie — the final expression of the destructive passions that have dominated Eve and Tyvian throughout. At the end of the flashback, Tyvian walks away from the bar, Branco following, to the Piazza San Marco, where Eve is sitting with her latest lover, a Greek with whom she is going for a cruise. Tyvian arranges to meet her, with a note of pleading in his voice, when she comes back: she replies, distantly, "If I come back," then adds, with a note of genuine affection in her voice, "Bloody Welshman." McCormick and Anna Maria, whose relationship has throughout been a counterpoint to the central relationship of the movie, have been strolling nearby, unnoticed by the others. Just as Eve and Tyvian have come to accept each other, Anna Maria and McCormick have come to accept the institution of marriage, despite the fact that McCormick has derided both it and his relationship with Anna Maria: the unity of their relationship derives from the fact that both seem to accept that there is something ridiculous about it. McCormick's refusal to take himself or his marriage seriously lends them both a certain strength. The camera looks down on the Piazza as Eve walks away with her Greek, then moves away again across the statuary to the tree of life.

The National Film Archive print of *Eve* is the only print preserved that at all conforms to Losey's conception of the film. Much footage is missing (some sequences have been shortened even compared with the print originally distributed in the United Kingdom), but the soundtrack is Losey's; the film contains something of what Losey wanted and nothing that he did not want. The following extracts from a letter by Losey protesting about certain cuts made in the print between when Losey saw it in Scandinavia and when it was purchased for the Archive give some indication of the missing footage.

"You are well aware that my interest in the print stemmed from the degree of its completeness and particularly the fact that its soundtrack was original (notably the score and the Anna Proclemer dubbing of Virna Lisi). The soundtrack was still the original and it is a large part of the justification for the expense and difficulty of getting the print and dupe negative here . . . A print I told them was virtually intact, and which was purchased by them in that belief, proves to have at least eighteen cuts not previously in it — these amount to 10-15 minutes of screen time (the print now runs 1 hr. 58 mins., which is almost down to the length of the print first shown in Paris). I cannot conceive who has made these cuts or why, because they follow no consistent pattern. In the first place let me make it very clear that I am not referring to lost frames where the print may have been broken and then spliced by a projectionist — such cuts I take for granted and the print on the whole is in good condition, but the cuts are quite large and some of them could be accounted for only on the basis of reducing the length of the film arbitrarily, or a few might be censorship cuts (but you had already shown the film, so the version I saw last January must have passed your censor . . .).

(1). The first establishing close-up of Jeanne Moreau on the barge in front of the Lido at Venice is missing. There are also two other cuts in the water-skiing sequence including the shot that establishes the Lido and makes the transition to the Venice Festival.

(2). The end of the seduction scene in Eve's flat in Rome, beginning with the shot of the goldfish aquarium, is deleted in its entirety.

(3). The first establishing sequence of the Jeanne Moreau flat in Venice has been entirely deleted, which means that when we return to the flat in one of the final sequences of the picture, we don't know where we are for quite some time.

(4). The scene which first establishes the island villa of the Stanley Baker character is very seriously damaged. It began with a 180 degree shot from the Torcello tower, panning across the landscape to the farm. This was perhaps the most beautiful shot in the picture and an important music cue. This cut has been made in the middle of the shot and, unlike the others, obviously and clumsily, and I am one hundred percent certain that this particular cut had not been made in the print I viewed. The rest of this sequence has been seriously vandalised, losing both the beginning and end long-shots of the two figures at the gate and the reflection of Moreau in the lagoon.

(5). There is a very skilful cut made in the gambling sequence which removes the main point of the sequence.

(6). The sequence that follows the gambling sequence, namely the arrival of the Moreau and Baker characters by boat in the dawn at their private wharf, has been entirely deleted. This arrival was in a circular sweep which was an important part of the movement of the sequence, and it also reprised the Torcello tower in the background; this and No. 4. above being preparations for the final shot of the Torcello tower in the last island sequence before the death of Virna Lisi. Apart from the beauty of this sequence, you may remember that the Baker character falls during it and rips his hand. Moreau laughs and he strikes her, knocking her down. She says "Only my husband can do that". The deletion of this scene leaves what follows entirely without motivation;

it also makes the bandage on Baker's hand in the subsequent sequence an irritating unexplained item.

(7). The sequence in the island villa bedroom which follows has been shortened (except for the reasons given above this cut could be explained as a censorship cut, although the cuts include a particularly beautiful end close-up of Moreau which could not be censorable. Other cuts involved were the shortening of two shots of Moreau, to eliminate brief exposure of her breast, and the shortening of Baker's exit from the bedroom) . . ."

16. The Servant

"THE LAST third of *The Servant* obviously was emotionally and aesthetically a paying off, and, if you like, a resolution (however negative) of the consequences of, the ultimate deterioration resulting from, living by false values — turning the relationship upside down to expose the falsity of values on both sides, a falsity leading, finally, to utter degradation and disaster for all concerned, excepting, perhaps, the rather incompletely drawn Susan, who simply flees from it, and probably retires into her own particular shell, in which she will find her own decay rapid. Not, perhaps, so degenerate . . .

"Every society has its false values, must have, and the question — I think the main question — is the degree to which people are free to explore them, combat them, change them. Theoretically democracy offers this opportunity, but more and more, as it hardens, as in the case of any society, these freedoms become less and less, and people's self-defences become greater, but the particular false values that exist in England are perhaps no greater or worse than those that exist elsewhere . . . The only thing that is worth anything, I think, is some individual consistency and purpose and sustained energy and examination of self and examination of the society one is living in. If you're going to talk about this — I don't mean talk — if you're going to deal with this in whatever your craft may be, or even in your individual life, it has to be from the basis of the society that you're in, that you know, and that you're observing, and I've been in England now some time and am part of it, and therefore this film was about England as *The Prowler* was about America." *Joseph Losey* (J.D.L.)

The camera frames a "By Appointment" sign, a symbol both of servility and of an outdated attitude to achievement, power and status, then draws back to reveal Hugo Barrett (the servant), dapper, respectable looking, standing outside the shop of Thomas Crapper Ltd., sanitary engineers to King George V (the movie treats, essentially, those aspects of existence which are usually not referred to, talked about; the "guilty secrets" of the individual and society). Barrett is about to cross fashionable King's Road, Chelsea. The particular relationship which the movie explores is a symbol of a whole country, a country which is dominated by outdated notions of its importance, and by an exhausting internecine strife. The self-centredness, sterility and ultimate decadence of a whole class is evoked through Tony and his friends of a previous generation, the Mountsets; that sterility has provoked the hostility of the class for which Barrett stands, a hostility that is expressed through a determination by the have-nots to live as comfortably and effortlessly as possible off the haves, a defensive reaction which may well be imposed on the have-nots by the arrogance of the haves, but which is ultimately self-defeating and self-destructive. The house in which the drama is acted out grows into a womb-like prison in which Tony and Barrett, master and servant, boss and worker, and, at times, homosexual couple in a sado-masochistic relationship, husband and wife (Barrett at one point nags Tony about his indolence in a world where the cost of living is continually rising), son and mother even (early on, Barrett cossets Tony like a mother, or a nanny, providing him with a protection from the harsh realities of life) are bound inseparably together by bonds of knowledge, hate, guilt and love from which they have not the strength of will to escape: "I wouldn't mind going out for a walk," says Tony wistfully, some time after Barrett's return, sitting quite motionless. The relationship between upper-class and lower-class in England is uncomfortably like that between white and negro in William Faulkner's vision of the South. Every so often, hatreds flare up (as in a strike); at one point, Barrett flares up: "I run the whole bloody place for you." The ambiguity of Losey's symbolism here results from no confusion on his part: he is expressing the underlying identity of all relationships — sexual, marital, economic, political — which involve servility or exploitation rather than the co-operative and collaborative efforts of free individuals. Such relationships are a refuge from the struggle of being alive; consequently addictions, such as Tony's ultimate alcoholism, drug-taking and sexual perversion, themselves escapes, evoke strikingly the degradation that is inherent in them. Thus *The Servant* lends itself to both a socio-political and a psycho-analytical interpretation. The pervasive visual motif of the film is the triangle: Barrett between Tony and Susan, between Tony and Vera (Barrett's voyeuristic presence arouses the social and sexual guilt of the other characters, none of whom have the strength to come to terms with this guilt); Tony's ancestors between him and Vera; most strikingly of all, in the pub scene where Barrett begs Tony to be allowed to return to his employment (a speech worthy of Strindberg's valet Jean, expressing a self-pitying vision of what it is like to be a have-not that plays on the guilt of the haves): though Barrett's tale may establish a certain masculine sympathy between himself and Tony, they are separated by the wall that divides the saloon bar from the public bar, a beautifully concise image of the

128

THE SERVANT: "I wouldn't mind going out for a walk." Tony (James Fox) and Barrett (Dirk Bogarde).

THE SERVANT: Barrett (Dirk Bogarde) has a self-pitying vision of what it is like to be a have-not.

KING AND COUNTRY. Above: Hamp (Tom Courtenay) and Hargreaves (Dirk Bogarde) at the court-martial. "Like you told me to say, I was acting under extraordinary strain." Below left: Webb (Barry Foster) and the Padre (Vivian Matalon). "I've laid on a couple of things myself which might be just as useful." Below right: Hamp, blindfolded, being carried through the firing-squad. "Nobody could aim at the moon in a situation like that."

traditional class division. Each pair in the movie is united and simultaneously separated by their social relationships.

Barrett crosses King's Road, and the camera moves back with him as he walks, purposefully, to the Royal Avenue house where he has an appointment with his future master, Tony. It follows him as he looks around the bare rooms of Tony's unfurnished house. Barrett finds Tony stretched out asleep ("It's too many beers at lunch, that's what it is," says Tony when he wakes, by way of explanation); Barrett gives a flicker of a smile, fleetingly knowing and superior. There is a brief passage of cross-cutting from the sleeping Tony to Barrett, who coughs deprecatingly to waken him; the camera frames Barrett, then zooms gently back to reveal Tony's expression for the first time: indolent, spoilt, weakly arrogant. The effect of the sequence (which beautifully integrates acting, cutting and camera-movement) is to give us a flash of awareness; it sums up the whole ensuing relationship. The same effect is achieved by the first sequence in which Tony and Susan (his girl-friend, or fiancée, who represents the possibility of a creative sexual and emotional relationship) are seen together in the house: Losey cuts fluidly from a close-up of Tony and Susan kissing to show, just as Tony's attention starts to wander from Susan, that they are lying on a pile of rugs and newspapers in a room in the unfurnished house. Tony gives expression to what is essentially a romantic, escapist dream — going to Brazil to work on a development project designed to alleviate the lot of the peasants of Asia Minor — and asks Susan to join him: he is not really interested in her (her remark — "Bachelor" — is a joking comment on his sexual failure), or in the unrealised potentialities of himself and his relationships that the room symbolises.

The essential class antagonisms are most clearly expressed in the relationship between Barrett and Susan, who is both a threat to Barrett (Tony, married to her, would be very different, and unlikely to employ Barrett) and, in a sense, a provocation: lacking the *savoir faire* that results from an upper-class background (her accent, and certain ignorance s — for example when Tony and Barrett, both out to impress, d isplay their knowledge of wine lore: Barrett, "Just a Beaujolais, s ir, but a good bottler"; Susan, "A good *what*?" — establish tha t she is not a member of the upper-class), she does not know ho w to handle Barrett. Though she is a positive force — consistently related to flowers, light, fresh air — she is cruelly insulting to B arrett, precisely because she, in turn, senses that he represents a threat to herself and Tony, a threat which she does not really u nderstand. She, too, stands for a class, the practical middle-class which, caught in the conflict between master and servant, adopts an extreme anti-worker attitude precisely because it lacks the near-feudal pretence of paternalistic concern that is a stock in trade of the upper classes. In this context, she is ineffectual because she acts too late, and with too limited knowledge.

Vera, Barrett's girl-friend, who does more or less what he tells her, and who seduces Tony, represents the brutalisation of sexual relationships in a society in which the individual is essentially dominated by his self-absorption. Barrett tells her at one point, "You're like a ruddy machine"; she replies, "I know I am, but I can't help it." Indeed, the "machine" has a certain fascination, representing sex without emotional responsibilities: as Vera says to Tony during the confrontation after he and Susan have found Vera and Barrett making love in his bed: "You can't 'ave it on a plate forever, can you?" Tony's attraction to Vera is essentially an obsession (the little scene in Nick's Diner, where Tony all the time is eyeing the waitress, who resembles Vera, establishes this, as does Tony's behaviour after Vera has left: at one point, he picks up a girl in a pub, then, later, we see him weeping with frustration on Vera's bed). He can be uninhibited with her, whereas he can't with Susan, whom he wants to marry, and whom he to some extent identifies with his mother: when she selects a chair on her first visit to the newly furnished apartment, he says with pride, "My mother's favourite." Susan does attempt a healthy criticism of Tony's pretensions and deceptions, but he is too hollow to respond to this; after he has broken down in the restaurant, he lacks the strength to make any reassessment of himself, and works out his inadequacy on Barrett with a burst of temper: "Damn awful lunch ... Where were you? ... Get me a brandy." The scene closes with a close-up of Tony, his brandy, his cigar: a complex image precisely because the shot is so beautiful, conveying both the attractiveness and inadequacy of Tony's way of life.

Vera, in turn, seems certainly to be attracted to Tony; in the seduction scene she is clearly as nervous as he is (she is nervous, too, when earlier she serves Tony his breakfast for the first time). Tony would obviously be, at least superficially, a rather exotic and attractive figure to someone in her position. When she begs him for help later in the movie, claiming that she really loved him and not Barrett, she, too, is making the speech which is most likely to arouse his compassion, but there is, perhaps, some truth in what she says: Tony, though obsessed with her, never gives any indication of contemplating a full, mature relationship with her; their class difference is too great. He offers her no positive alternative to the sexuality that Barrett represents, and even Barrett gives her some happiness and enjoyment.

The dominant force in this microcosm of the world is guilt: Barrett is successful precisely because he plays on the fears and guilts of the other characters, who try to avoid confrontations at all costs. One of the most beautiful images in the movie comes during the seduction scene in the kitchen: Tony and Vera are face to face; a tap is dripping loudly; Losey cuts in a close-up of the dripping tap — a concise image of Tony's actual physical condition at this moment; Tony, seeking to repress or deny the physiological forces that are at the root of the human personality, turns the tap sharply to stop the sound of dripping, but then the ticking of a clock takes up the same excited pulse-beating rhythm. (A superb use of non-naturalistic sound.) However hard one tries to repress one's sexuality, it cannot be denied; if one channel of expression is denied to it, it will find another. (A West Coast critic, deliberately misinterpreting the imagery and theme of the film, found something to snicker at in this scene: sex-guilt may be irrelevant and outdated on the West Coast, but it's still a pretty potent factor in human relationships elsewhere).

The restaurant scene provides an extension into "normal" society of the points established during the film. The three couples are all trapped in relationships in which there is no contact, no genuine human sympathy. The bishop dominates the curate by virtue of position and authority; the older woman dominates (or attempts to) in what seems to be a lesbian relationship by virtue of age and aggressive intensity; the society man (played by Harold Pinter, who wrote the script) establishes himself in his relationship with the girl by means of his ingratiating personality. On one occasion, Losey cuts back to Tony and Susan from a bitterly intense conversation between the two women. A moment later we see the two women in the background, apparently behaving quite normally. This moment provides a beautiful comment on Losey's art. He is not interested in the superficial appearance of a relationship, its naturalistic surface, but in its deep, inner reality. When he examines a relationship, it is this that he shows; when a relationship is no longer in the forefront of his concern, he shows it as it would appear to an external observer.

Just as some of Shakespeare's finest work is about the distinction between "seeming" and "being" (for example *Hamlet*, or *Othello* even), so *The Servant* is essentially about "seeming." I find that I could have used the verb "seem" repeatedly in my discussion of the movie; in a world in which characters lack a genuine independent identity, one does not know what the motives, emotions, personalities of the characters *are*. This comes across very forcibly in, say, the interviews in the issue of *Isis* devoted to *The Servant* (and to some extent in the interview with Losey in *Film* 38); no-one, not Losey, not Pinter, not the actors, can say for certain *why* somebody behaves as he does; they can only offer their personal reactions and interpretations, and Losey's interpretation is hardly more valid than anybody else's. In a world dominated by guilt, no-one can see clearly what the truth *is;* there are no educable characters in the movie, no-one learns to see clearly. The only positives the movie hints at, apart from those associated with the ineffectual Susan, who, as she flees at the end, has obviously been deeply marked by her experience, are the job-sense of the workmen decorating the house (who hold Barrett in contempt for his fussiness) and the stoical reaction to misfortune of the man in the pub ("I had a bit of bad luck today"), both of which are purely instinctive and non-intellectualised. This apart, the sardonic humour of the dialogue is all that relieves the movie's almost obsessive progress to the climax of the "orgy". Thus the truth which *The Servant* conveys is the truth which results from the dialectic between the movie and the individual members of the audience; the only clarity of vision that it expresses is the clarity of vision of the individual spectator which may result from his viewing the movie. *The Servant* is an essentially Brechtian work.

17. King and Country

"I WANTED to do the film when I realised how many millions
of people had died in that war — I've forgotten what the exact
figure is; I think several hundred thousand men simply disappeared
into the mud . . . They went and went and went; and all they knew
was "King and Country", the particular shibboleth of the moment.
And the shibboleths appear in various forms. And now it's become
so bloody cynical that a politician can change his particular set of
shibboleths between an election campaign and three months after
his election, and nobody takes him up on it. He doesn't even seem
to take himself up on it . . .

"I think a lot of people find the film just impossible to take in
horror, and this I understand, and this I accept. I don't think it's
right, but I accept it . . .

"I was consciously attempting to give myself a discipline — in
the case of this picture it was, in a sense, a necessary discipline, because the picture could not have been made unless it was made for
a particular budget, and since I found the subject a claustrophobic
one, I attempted to stay within the Greek unities of time and place,
and to make it absolutely austere. As you know, there's only one
set. It was a composite set, and we never go outside of that set. I
think that the Greek chorus, which was also conscious, fails.
King and Country fails partially because it's a bit too self-conscious
and partially because it perhaps isn't well enough written, a very
hard thing to write. It also fails probably because I was trying very
hard to make the point that in that war, towards the end of that
war, the bulk of the people who were being killed were very young.
They were under twenty, and the chorus was therefore very young.
However, what I was getting around to saying was that the scene
that was most attacked in *King and Country* is the one that I most

like, and the one that I think is most successful, and that I most enjoyed doing, which is, if you like, the so-called "orgy" before the execution, in which I wanted to get the sense of human creatures clinging to flesh, to each other's flesh, and to the preservation of their own flesh, and attempting to comfort, and at the same time being hideously cruel, by mocking the thing that is going to happen, and by a very strange mixture of 'I must survive no matter what happens to the other guy, and yet I want to comfort him, and I want him to forget what's going to happen to him, and I want somehow to forget that it may be me tomorrow, and it might perfectly well have been me today.' And, if you like, this is a stylised scene, but the whole picture is to some extent stylised. But I find it the truest and most emotional thing in the film, and I hoped that it would serve to make it unmistakably clear, when the actual execution occurred, that none of these men, in the somewhat sober dawn, coming an hour or so after this affair, would want to kill the man. But nobody could aim at the moon in a situation like that without being shot himself."

"Why does Hargreaves kill him, and not Webb, who's in charge of the firing-squad?"

"Hargreaves kills him, because it seemed to me that, dramatically and emotionally, it was essential, since Hargreaves approached the job as a duty that was distasteful, with an attitude that the man was essentially guilty, and that, in this kind of situation, if a man violates the rules, you shoot him and the whole ritual of trial is nonsense. But, in the course of the contact with this man as a human being, he came to certain realisations about this man, and about Man, and about himself, which made it obligatory for him to complete the faith which the boy had given him by personally putting him out of his misery, and because, at the moment when that bullet is fired, Hargreaves himself is dead. I mean it's no longer going to be possible for that man to hide from himself . . ."

"I find the colonel a very complex character; on one level, he's a father-figure to his officers . . . "

"The father-figure is a man who's reached the point of conformity, which many people do reach, where he says 'This is how it is. I can't change it, and what can I do about it?' And, when he's directly confronted with the question 'Do you believe it's right? Do you *know* whether it does any good?' he says he doesn't. And, in fact, he doesn't. But in fact the terms that he's come to with himself and with society are such that, whether he knows it's right or not, he's going to do it because he personally doesn't want to make the battle. You may ask somebody whether they believe in segregation or race prejudice, or war, or whatever, and they may absolutely not believe, and know that they don't believe, but they personally are not going to accept the responsibility of doing anything about it, because they believe they can't, and because they wish to survive . . .

"I think that there are people who do act differently in these situations. Obviously, there are people who in many situations have stood up, and been victims of their standing up, or, sometimes, they've come out of it not victims but survivors. But the people who choose to do that, understandably, are few. And the situations which turn out that way are few. I suppose it could be said, well, why not deal with one of these situations, and I would say that the reason for not dealing with one of these situations is because we've had enough heroes and there are few heroes, and this is not the problem . . .

"The cut-ins were a stylistic thing which I thought would work. It seemed to me essential to give almost subliminal flashes of the kind of thing which Hamp had come from, which were not intended to be exact. They were not memories, and they were not realistic reproductions, but they were a combination of memory and fantasy and reality. Many people haven't even observed them, they've had their effect without being commented on, which is pleasing when it happens." *Joseph Losey* (J.D.L.)

"Dulce et decorum est pro patria mori." *Sir Gerald Tarrant* (after Horace) in *Modesty Blaise*.

As so often with Losey's major films, the opening shot of *King and Country* reveals the point of view of the director, and the essential theme of the movie. Losey takes his camera in really close to the Royal Artillery war memorial, making the spectator *see* something essentially very different from the reminder of past glory that registers on the consciousness when one walks casually past the memorial: the usually unnoticed detail of the memorial evokes with overwhelming power the grimness, death, exhaustion that war involves. On the soundtrack, there is the sound of Hamp's mouth-organ, his only means of self-expression or articulateness. Slowly the roar of traffic fades in, gradually growing louder and louder. The camera, by taking us closer, shows us the grim,truthful reality behind the vague image of heroism that the monument evokes; the soundtrack links the past horror ("which now seems hundreds of years away, and having nothing to do with us" — *Joseph Losey* [J.D.L.]) with the present lack of concern with the lessons of the past that is a vital ingredient of the attitude of these who casually pass or drive by the monument. Losey cuts abruptly from the stone gun of the monument to a shell-explosion from stock footage, then a close track across the mud of the Front — rain, trenches, cans: the paraphernalia of war. Then still photographs of the war, whilst Hamp's voice recites lines of Housman's war poetry: "Life, to be sure, is nothing much to lose" — an articulation which Hamp himself could not make, and which takes on an ambiguity precisely because it is placed in Hamp's mouth. Losey dissolves from a skull which has almost disappeared into the mud to Hamp's face as he lies playing his mouth-organ.

The use of the RA monument (Hamp is an infantryman) immediately implies that Losey's condemnation is of the whole war-machine, and of the society that produced it, the illusions that allowed it to be produced. War involves the creation of a machine in which there is no longer any question of individual responsibility; a whole society is indicted for its complicity, as the cut in of King George V and the Kaiser when Hamp answers Hargreaves's question "Why did you volunteer?" with the slogan "King and Country" implies. The fusion of past and present that Losey achieves through his soundtrack establishes that such an indictment of a past society necessarily implies an indictment of any present society that sees the past as mistily and unclearly as ours does: our image of the Great War (the very name we know it by is a give-away; it was *Great* only for the number of victims it claimed) is as blurred and confused as Hamp's images of his background, the mixture of fantasy, memory and reality that determined his actions and his fate. The very title of the movie, *King and Country*, arouses an image of screen gallantry instead of the brutal reality of war. The letter of condolence read at the end, from the Secretary of the War Office, clinches the irony: if Hamp must die ingloriously at the Front to encourage his fellows, those at home must, in turn, be fed the illusion of the glory that death in war involves, an illusion reinforced by the full-dress regalia of the Kings and generals whose pictures are cut or dissolved in at certain points, a sad contrast to the muddy reality of the war. The cynical comments about their service of Hamp's fellow soldiers echo this gap between what society *believes* and what war *is:* "The perfect soldier . . . loved his country . . . killed the Kaiser . . . won the war"; unlike most of his mates, Hamp was a volunteer: his confused idealism making him less adapted for survival than they are. Hamp says of his mates sadly: "I suppose they think I've let 'em down," but Sparrow expresses his more realistic point of view: "I wouldn't have been ni Hamp's shoes. If I'd done it, I wouldn't have got caught." Hamp throughout is, as Hargreaves describes him, "embarrassingly honest", too confused to look after himself, lacking the cynical cunning of his mates: the perfect scapegoat for their fears, and confirmation that they, somehow, are different. Yet, clearly they are not; after Hamp's execution the unit will return to the Front, and any who die will be commemorated with the same letter of condolence. "A proper court is concerned with law. It's a bit amateur to plead for justice," Captain Midgley, the prosecuting officer, tells Captain Hargreaves after the trial; within the frame-work of the war-machine, human distinctions are blurred; Lieutenant Webb's description of Hamp as a "first class" soldier, who "brewed a good cup of tea", is as valid an epitaph as any. In the claustrophobic world of the army, of trench-warfare, Webb's empiricism, which expresses an instinctive concern for the men under his command, is the only positive force that has any hope of survival, and even Webb can do nothing to help Hamp. "You going to get the silly bastard off?" he asks Hargreaves hopefully before the trial, "I'll perjure myself for the man, if you like." When he does attempt to help Hamp whilst giving evidence, he is neatly ensnared by Midgley's cross-examination, and ends by protesting: "I've said what I believe." Though he had shown Hamp the sympathy the doctor had denied him, his remedy was not likely to be more help: the doctor gave him laxative pills ("The one thing I didn't have any need of was a No. 9," Hamp says in his pre-trial interview with Hargreaves, causing him to smile sympathetically, touching him for the first time), while Webb gave him extra rum. But, as Midgley points out, Webb did not suggest that Hamp be taken out of the line. Webb's claim that Hamp must have been suffering from greater strain than his fellows because he deserted is as unreasoning as the doctor's comment that Hamp's desertion proves him right in his diagnosis that Hamp's condition "was a case of cold feet." The positives that are suggested by the character of the well-meaning Webb are severely qualified by this ineffectuality. Certainly, later in the movie, he states a compassionate rationalist humanist case that engages the spectator's sympathy, but even he has nevertheless been involved in the general complicity, despite the fact that his actions later on are designed to make Hamp's last night on earth bearable. When the padre prepares to give Hamp communion, Webb asks: "Is he very religious?", then adds, referring to the injection he intends to give Hamp, "I've laid on a couple of things myself which might be just as useful. I've spoken to the C.O., it's left to his discretion, and he's left it to me." Unlike the C.O., who passes the buck here, just as he did earlier (after the verdict, he was able either to confirm the sentence which the court passed on Hamp, or send to higher authority for approval; he chose to do the latter, and his superiors insisted on the death-sentence which the court-martial had decided against), Webb is willing to accept responsibility for a humanitarian gesture. Webb and the padre go to Hamp, interrupting the "orgy" during which Hamp and his mates seek oblivion with stolen rum, an oblivion which is not to be found: the other soldiers end up by tormenting Hamp cruelly, blindfolding him, and having a mock execution: violence and death are too close to be blotted out of the consciousness. Whilst the padre mouths the words of the communion service, "The body of our Lord Jesus Christ, which was given for thee . . . ", Hamp takes a deep, desperate swig of the communion wine, hoping that drink will blot out everything, but the body rebels before the mind has reached the oblivion it is seeking: Hamp vomits up the alcohol he has consumed. Webb injects the sedative, with the help of the padre, who at first had seemed somewhat disapproving of the idea that a sedative be used: "Where's the soul, padre?" Webb asks; "Here, "the padre replies; Webb comments: "All that's here is a few hours of bloody nothing" — a few hours of oblivion before death, which is for Webb, the final, total oblivion.

The core of the film is the relationship between Hamp and Captain Hargreaves — "Soldier's friend." "He's no idea what might happen to him," the corporal who arrested Hamp tells Hargreaves; Hamp seems to be in a state of shock which is not so much his defence against war in general as his defence against the possibility of execution; he reacts during his trial as if he were a spectator watching something which did not concern him, smiling, like the colonel, at the doctor's threat to Hargreaves over laxative pills: "I'll prescribe them for you in a minute." His attempt to walk to England is, as Hargreaves describes it, "a hopeless, desperately stupid thing," not the action of a man responsible for his actions; Hamp "might just as well have tried to clear a German trench single-handed"; such a response to intolerable pressure would have been equally out of contact with the reality of the situation. Hamp says of his desertion: "It was like a dream, sir." That Hamp is an extreme case of a condition general to all the soldiers is clearly established by the behaviour of some of his fellows, many of whom seem almost in a daze; their uneasy sleep, the hysteria which seems always there just below the surface (at one point, a soldier flicks a rat off his bunk on to Sparrow; the rat bites Sparrow, who becomes almost hysterical with pain and anger; a soldier cries out wildly during his sleep; another babbles: "This ground will grow no more buttercups.") evoke the atmosphere of war as clearly as do the whines of distant shells on the soundtrack. In this condition, Hamp turns to his officers, as father-figures, as if he hoped they could magically alleviate the situation; he hoped the doctor would be able to give him a tonic, or something to make him sleep, or stop his diarrhoea; whereas the cunning Sparrow would make a good malingerer, Hamp is too honest to have any success; he needs a gesture of help to relax the pressure on him, but, though he does not realise it, the only help he could receive would be to be sent home. As Hargreaves says at the trial, "A man can only take so much"; Hamp is no malingerer; it is just that his *body* rebelled, actively, though his mind was too dazed to do so. When he starts to tell Hargreaves about the death of his mate, Willie, he has another attack of diarrhoea. After his arrest, Hamp turns to Hargreaves as he had turned to Webb and the doctor for help, but is still unable to grasp the reality of the situation: "You can believe me. It'll come out all right," he tells Hargreaves; "They can't shoot me," Hamp says, because nobody else in A-company has been out as long as he has. He believes naïvely in the good will of his officers, that they are kindly and sympathetically disposed towards him: "I'd like to thank you, sir," he tells Hargreaves on their first meeting, "It's not as though you have to do it." In fact, Hargreaves has not chosen to defend Hamp out of any sympathy; for him, it is a duty, an unpleasant duty; he's already told Webb: "He's failed . . . If a dog breaks its back . . . you shoot it." Hargreaves rejects Hamp's thanks by telling him he should be standing at attention; he sees him not as a fellow human being, someone whose feelings and emotions he might himself share, but as an object of contempt. War, for him, is a test of a man's worth: "We're all on trial for our life," he has told Webb. Hamp evokes for Hargreaves an image of war and death that he has blotted out of his mind: "The fellows I came out with, there's none of 'em left except me"; Losey cuts in an image of death, then dissolves back to Hargreaves and Hamp: this particular cut-in seems to refer to the consciousness of Hargreaves rather than that of Hamp. Hargreaves is suddenly very tense and disturbed, but left alone when Hamp is escorted to the latrine, he rejects the corporal's second attempt to establish contact with him — "I told you he was a strange one, sir," — with an order, "Attend to that, will you," pointing to a skeleton in the trench that his hand had brushed against. However, during the interview with Hamp, Hargreaves's sympathies start to be engaged. Hamp has derived from his experiences a logic as unanswerable as the logic of the military: Hargreaves asks him how he would have felt if his fellows had run off, leaving him alone during a battle; "I don't think it could have been much worse." He tells Hargreaves: "I didn't have a plan. I ain't got the sense, have I?" Hargreaves asks Hamp if he were sent to a military prison, could he be relied upon to do his duty when he came out; Hamp replies: "Do I have to tell you the truth, sir? Can *you* tell me, sir?" He later silences Midgley's cross-examination about his desertion by protesting: "I've never done this before, sir. This was the first time."

It is too simple to say that contact with Hamp provokes a conflict between Hargreaves the officer, part of the military machine, and Hargreaves the man. At the start of the movie, the officer was defending Hamp because it was his duty to do so, whereas the man had already condemned him. Hargreaves's first conversation with Webb makes it clear that his inhumanity dates from before he joined the army: he embodies an attitude deeply ingrained in society at large; his choice of profession is an expression of his attitude towards life in general, an attitude which sees life and human behaviour in terms of clearcut black and white moral judgments, judgments that totally ignore the complexity of human behaviour and experience. The army, with its discipline, its chain of command, its machine-like efficiency, is based on just such a denial of human complexity and needs. However, in his role as an officer, Hargreaves is forced into realisation of his common humanity with Hamp, and his responsibilities as a man: his duty as an officer leads directly to the human contact that shatters his inhuman protective shell (again, one of the central Losey images: the man who is trapped by his very attempts to evade or deny his human obligations). Once that shell has started to crack, there is a peculiar ambiguity about

143

Hargreaves's behaviour, as if he no longer knew what to deny, what to affirm. His speech to the court-martial is melodramatic, theatrical, as if his emotions had been frozen for so long that he cannot properly express them: every gesture is timed, every pause studied, every outburst of passion calculated. He is presenting an emotional or idealistic case, but cannot be truly emotional — his logical intellect remains strangely in control of his actions. His behaviour certainly alienates his colonel, the presiding officer. "No, no, no," the colonel exclaims as Hargreaves gets too theatrical in his cross-examination of the doctor; "You've made your point," he comments abruptly later, cutting Hargreaves short. Hargreaves's closing speech emphasises Hamp's lack of responsibility for his own actions, the fact that Hamp has been out here "longer than some of us", that people no longer ask why the war is being fought, that unlike Hamp, the court is able to *choose:* "This court *is* responsible for its actions . . . He volunteered because his wife and his mother dared him . . . Are we not fighting to preserve for this court the right to choose?" When Hargreaves concludes by stating that if justice is not done by the court, men are dying for nothing, the colonel quietly but angrily comments: "Matter of opinion."

Hargreaves represents more, here, than just an officer trying to defend a prisoner; he is making articulate the needs of inarticulate humanity, yet, precisely because he is so logical and articulate in his approach to life, he cannot completely succeed in convincing his fellow officers of the sincerity of his plea, and thus of the genuineness of Hamp's case. He senses this, and, in his final confrontation with the colonel, asks whether he failed in his presentation of the case; "I did my best," he says pathetically; "Very eloquent," the colonel remarks drily; his plea has essentially been a performance, for which he receives the plaudits of his fellows, all of them, Midgley included, hoping that he will get Hamp off; thus he

MODESTY BLAISE: Top, Sir Gerald Tarrant (Harry Andrews), Willie Garvin (Terence Stamp) and Modesty Blaise (Monica Vitti). Tarrant: "If you'd been a bit late . . ." Willie: "Yeah, well, somebody had to take a chance, and I'm chicken." Below, "Your Mr. Garvin is going to help us, otherwise . . . Oh, no, I can't say it, it's pure melodrama." Clara Fothergill (Rossella Falk), Gabriel (Dirk Bogarde), Willie (Terence Stamp) and Modesty (Monica Vitti).

MODESTY BLAISE. Modesty (Monica Vitti): "You know, Willie, we should have." Willie (Terence Stamp): "It's less common this way."

hasn't truly engaged their sympathies, made them share the knowledge he has shared: his performance has been too controlled, which is dangerous.

Artistically *King and Country* is one of the most *controlled* pleas for humanity ever made, whilst at the same time it expresses the dangers of such artistic control. Hargreaves, when confronting the colonel, has at last become so involved that he is running the risk of losing sight of his own life, of cracking up. He is pathetic — he has just come from seeing Hamp, and was there when the sentence was read out; Hamp collapsed on his knees when he heard the news, and Hargreaves, who had just once again rejected Hamp's gratitude by rounding savagely on him for his failure to do his duty, was obviously moved to real compassion; Losey's cutting and camera-positions placed both Hamp and Hargreaves together, on the receiving end of the sentence — and dirty, having just fallen in the mud. The colonel reprimands him: "Rather short on ceremony, aren't we?"; "Yes, sir, I had too much of that today"; "You lost," the colonel replies, as if it had been a game; "We all lost . . . We're all bloody murderers." The colonel tells him to pull himself together. "Pull yourself together, pull yourself together, you're talking like the bloody doctor!"; "Aren't we rather overstepping?" the Colonel asks. Hargreaves challenges him: "A technical desertion . . . Just a little walk. And you *know* it." He wants to know: "Has it ever encouraged anyone, or discouraged anyone?"; the Colonel says he believes it has. "Are you sure?" Hargreaves asks; "Not quite," the colonel replies; there is a glance of communication, of momentary sympathy, exchanged between them. Hargreaves becomes calmer as the Colonel talks of the way in which his decisions are dominated by "necessity", as if the Colonel's moment of self-questioning, of doubt, had given him strength, a strength perhaps resulting from the knowledge that others had shared his disillusionment. When Hargreaves leaves the Colonel he is again in command of his emotions; he sees the "party" that is going on where Hamp is confined, pauses, as if not knowing what to do, then decides to ignore it, behaviour rather different from that of the old Hargreaves.

Whilst Hamp is being tried, his fellow privates stage a mock trial of the rat that bit Sparrow's ear; or, rather, making the parallel more ironic, the one rat which they catch when they go on a hunt beating the side of a dead mule to drive out a horde of rats. Hamp is an arbitrary scapegoat for the fears of all of them; their treatment of him in the final "orgy" may well give an indi-cation of their attitude to him generally; certainly, he seems a bit apart from his fellows, who are unlikely to have shown him much constructive help and sympathy. Their behaviour is part of the total atmosphere of war from which he fled. One interpretation[13] suggests that this is the key to the whole movie: Hamp fled from the homosexuality of his comrades. There is certainly a current of homosexuality in the behaviour of the soldiers — their sentimental, and very physical comforting of Hamp: "There's no disgrace," some lines of dialogue, but such veiled homosexuality is typical of young men of that age in this kind of confined situation. There is, too, some homosexual imagery, and the administering of the in-jection reminds one, perhaps, of a violent homosexual contact which can lead to a form of oblivion, but to say that the movie is *about* homosexuality, or even that homosexuality is a central theme, is ridiculous. It is true, however, as Gottleib's interpretation argues, that *fear* is a dominant theme of the movie, but the fear, essentially, is the fear of death; the flesh, drink, drugs, sexual contact, can lead to an oblivion which blots out the fear of the final oblivion. So, too, can destructive violence — the execution of a scapegoat, be that scapegoat Hamp or a rat. In this world, where life is Hobbesian, "nasty, brutish, short", an inarticulate man can easily be trapped,

[13] Stephen Gottleib: *Film Culture* No. 40, Spring 1966.

like a rat, and the rat, by being a substitute victim, can replace a man. There is no suggestion that change or development is possible, at least not within the war-machine, and as Losey has indicated in *The Criminal* and *The Damned*, the logic of efficiency, of the war-machine, is being applied to society at large. Even Bannion, though confronted with hell, achieves a certain freedom in his moment of dying: he struggles out to the centre of the field where he has buried the loot, drawing Carter after him, thus ensuring that Suzanne may escape. For Hamp, death will be preceded by "a few hours of bloody nothing." Though Hamp's fellows don't want to kill him, they can't save him: it is almost as if Losey had chosen to *unwrite* Eisenstein's *Battleship Potemkin*, by giving expression to the British system, a system which seems unlikely to be changed by revolution (as Eisenstein himself commented once[14]). Losey is not conscious of any links with *Potemkin*, yet the execution scene is vaguely similar — the soldiers *don't* fire on their mate. Losey's privates also handle meat early in the movie, but, significantly, they keep the best cut for themselves, leaving the rest for their officers (the authentic spirit of the British Army); even the cut from the stone-gun to an explosion at the start of the movie is almost Eisensteinian. By expressing his attitude to the problems of human existence, Losey incidentally produces a refutation of Eisenstein; the parallels are accidental, the result of working with material which bears a loose resemblance to Eisenstein's. For Losey, a movie such as *Potemkin* would probably seem false in its suggestion that humanity can be changed by revolution (probably only shibboleths are changed by revolution) and perhaps over-calculated in its effects, too much the creation of a mind such as that of Hargreaves.

[14] "On another day they journeyed to Windsor to see the castle and Eton. 'Now I know why there will never be a revolution in England,' said Eisenstein". *Sergei M. Eisenstein* – a biography by Marie Seton. p. 146.

At the end of the film, when the firing-squad aim off, refusing to kill their mate (again, their attempt at kindness becomes cruelty), Hargreaves is dominated by his sense of duty to Hamp as a man, not as an officer. He pushes past the reluctant Webb, who, as officer in charge of the firing-squad, is the officer whose *duty* it is to kill Hamp, cradles his head in his arms, asks, "Isn't it finished yet?"; "No, sir; I'm sorry," Hamp replies: he has now learnt from Hargreaves what duty is, and feels he has failed once again in his duty by not dying cleanly and simply. Hargreaves places his pistol in Hamp's mouth, and pulls the trigger; Hamp's limbs twitch and stiffen as Hargreaves walks away; Losey "freezes" the frame, Hamp's feet in the foreground, an image that is a reprise of the still photographs used throughout the movie, and the sculpture of the war memorial. Hargreaves's (not Webb's) voice is heard reading the letter of condolence.

18. Modesty Blaise

"IN A SENSE, it was a kind of purgative thing for me, but I don't think that *Modesty Blaise* is the picture that most people are taking it to be, and I believe that, with a little bit of perspective it will be seen, in its own way, to make its comment on a particularly empty and hideous era of our century. This was the intention. But there are so many comments within *Modesty*, disguised in ways that I thought . . . not very much disguised, but presented in ways that I had thought would be reasonably palatable. I thought it could be taken at different levels. And I think it can. I'm told, by the way, that most teenagers are crazy about it, young people in college, and outside. It was intended for the young of mind and spirit. It's a bitter film, *Modesty Blaise*. It's probably the mixture of bitterness and humour and gaiety, and the fact that it was intended to work at several levels, that puts people off... It's full of violence — the picture is full of violence. Of course! But I have tried to use the alienation thing in every instance to do two things: one, to stop any enjoyment of violence as violence, at the point where it might have been enjoyed sadistically, and the other to make clear the utter, callous, cold-blooded acceptance of violence which is typical of our society, of our audiences, of our critics, and of our leaders. And to show that there is no value put on human life, and that killing is indiscriminate... There is no violence that isn't almost immediately mocked...

"The picture has been exploited, in my opinion, and in the opinion of many of the people who were involved in it, in a most incredibly wrong way. The audience was told that this was a woman who was 'more dangerous than the male'... a kind of female James Bond. To exploit it sensationally and vulgarly as something it isn't, obviously gets the wrong audience, and obviously precipitates a certain kind of unthinking critical response. If it's just another one in the series of what I consider these filthy pictures, filthy in their effect, and abominably made and styleless — this is part of their effect and success — then of course it won't work...

"I think the score does an enormous amount for the film, and it does, in its way, exactly what I was trying to do with the image, which was to make sounds which can be taken at various levels... It has a wide range, from the intentionally banal and the intentionally violent through the lyrical and beautiful. I think it's one of the most remarkable film scores I know, and it has not had one word of appreciation."

"Why don't Modesty and Willie sleep together? They talk about it."

"Some of the things that have come out, I think, particularly well in *Modesty Blaise* came about almost as improvisations to

149

meet the objections of the people who control the copyright who, among other things, insisted on the virginal relationship of Modesty and Willie, so I made capital of that."

"People who are very close in some ways often have a fear of getting sexually involved."

"Well, there was that intention, too. And, as a matter of fact, very often you may have an enormous attraction to people that you work with closely, and at the same time you know perfectly well, instinctively, that if you ever finally go to bed it will end the thing that you value, and that's working, and this was one of the things I consciously tried to do between the two of them. I don't think it works, frankly, and as one critic said, they acted as if they'd never been introduced. And I think this was so. They acted as if they'd never been introduced, really, and I hadn't been introduced to them." *Joseph Losey* (J.D.L.)

Modesty Blaise is an essentially *anti* film; it is anti, certainly, those targets that it obviously aims at — politicians and military leaders for example; three times master-criminal Gabriel parodies their statements: "I'm not a dessicated calculating machine . . ."; "I've given them the tools, they must finish the job"; "A good general weeps when he is forced to send his troops into action, and the tears of the widows . . . widows 'n' orphans . . . are his tears, too." Sir Gerald Tarrant is very upset when Modesty and the Sheik prepare to fire the presentation cannon the Sheik has given Modesty out of the window of the hotel; the window points towards Buckingham Palace. He's quite happy, though, when they take the cannon to another window. At one point, he uses a dead body as a decoy, to lure one of Gabriel's men into a trap. Like the poetry-quoting colonel in *King and Country*, Sir Gerald retreats into traditional cliché when the plane carrying the fake diamonds is shot down: "Dulce et decorum est pro patria mori", whilst

150

Gabriel, who gave the order for the rocket to be fired, and who has been listening in to the pilots' conversation, says: "Why can't they be bachelors?", then sighs with relief when he hears the pilots' parachutes have opened. In fact, Gabriel knows the plane was not carrying the real diamonds, as does his figure-conscious Scottish assistant (who *is*, according to Gabriel, "a dessicated calculating machine"), who comments: "We wasted a million on that wretched rocket"; Gabriel replies: "One has to do what one is expected to do." Whereas, in the average war-movie, a handful of men are set a task vital for the whole army, here two decoys are shot down by the pressing of a button, and what is at stake is not the safety of an army, or any worthwhile cause, but a financial transaction. Diamonds (an implied reference to the prevailing attitude to South Africa?), oil-concessions, these, not the sanctity or quality of human life, are what prevail in the world of Tarrant, his boss the Minister (whose ignorance of those he is seeking to make a treaty with has, repeatedly, to be corrected by Tarrant, and Modesty), and the Sheik, who wears an M.C.C. tie, and who sits in the desert reading *Hansard* and laughing uncontrollably: the morality of the politician is the morality of the master-criminal, and war is no more moral than gang warfare. Gabriel himself, respectably enough, reads *The Financial Times*.

Gabriel, the embodiment of ruthlessness, is at the same time the embodiment of the most commonplace notions of conventional middle-class sentimentality: "I can't bear to hear them scream," he says as his lobsters are dropped into boiling water; just before he orders the rocket-base to shoot down the plane carrying the false diamonds, he gives an "Oh!" of horror when he hears the pilot's childhood reminiscences: "When I was a child, my parents took me tobogganing." "How can I eat lobster when the lobsters are eating Borg?" he says, pushing his plate away, when he hears that one of the safe-crackers he has in training for an attempt on the vault of the *Tyboria* (which contains the real diamonds) has failed a diving test; McWhirter has no such scruples, and tucks in to Gabriel's leavings happily (as he does throughout the movie: Gabriel, who is repeatedly served the most exquisite of gourmet dishes, is repeatedly too fastidious to eat them). Gabriel watches fascinated whilst his associate, "Dear Clara Fothergill" ("a roaring psychopath", he calls her at one point) strangles Crevier, a clown who gave information to one of Tarrant's agents; in the audience for this performance by Mrs. Fothergill there is, too, McWhirter, who is always summoned to bring his ledgers on such occasions, to give an account of the financial state of the organisation. He keeps sneaking sly looks at the scene, and Gabriel kicks him, to make him pay attention to his accounts: McWhirter always argues, on financial grounds, against victims being brought back alive to Mrs. Fothergill, though, in fact, he seems to enjoy her displays. The tame friar they have in their stronghold watches Crevier's murder, mesmerised; later, he is easily lured into Modesty's cell by the sight of her bare leg beckoning from behind a door, and, when the stronghold has been captured by the Sheik, he is quite happy to join in the prayers to Allah: Christianity coming to terms with the modern world.

Gabriel is prepared to embark on a space programme if necessary; a criminologist argues that Gabriel (who is believed dead at the start of the movie) was not a true criminal, for "His only motive was malice" — the motive of the dead Mabuse, for example; but Lang's Mabuse is not dead, he lives on in Losey's Gabriel, who is repeatedly identified with the modern politician: the attitude towards politics implied is the bitterly disillusioned attitude of Barbara Garson's *Macbird*, but the total frame of reference of the movie is far wider than that of *Macbird*. *Modesty Blaise* is a movie of moods, changing abruptly from the bitter to the satirical to the lyrical. These changes of moods imply a life beyond that of politics: though Modesty's attitude is determined by an Eve-like desire to collect money, and not to be bettered, she does convey a certain enjoyment of life; the satiric gaiety of her flight from her pursuers in the Old Market of Amsterdam is a complex burlesque which defines Losey's attitude towards a whole genre: he creates the eerie atmosphere and suspense preceding the murder of Nicole better than anybody now working in the suspense genre (except for Hitchcock); then, having proved himself a master at treating this genre with style, burlesques it completely by transforming the chase into a Mack Sennett chase, with Mack Sennett music on the soundtrack. Nicole, the "canary" whom Willie hoped might "sing", is chased though the Old Market; there are notices saying "Jesus saves" hanging amongst suspended puppets which look down on the Market, but Jesus does not save Nicole: she is stabbed and her lifeless body thrown on a pile of old sacks, like a straw dummy. She gasps her last words to Modesty: "Tell Willie . . . Gabriel" — the information Willie and Modesty had required. Willie's women are loyal to him, but he is loyal only to Modesty, "The dream you never found." Just as Gabriel never eats any of the sumptuous dishes served to him, so Willie never lays any of the sumptuous dishes he gets into bed with: Modesty always needs him just at the crucial moment: "She knows. She's got an instinct for it." When interrupted the first time, he hurls a knife at a target across from his bed as his negro-girl leaves: frustrated sexuality finding its expression in meaningless violence. The gesture is repeated when he hurls his knife at Nicole's killer.

Modesty ("She is the perfect mistress of her art/She is the perfect mistress too"), though one of her lovers (Hagan) would not be surprised if she could control her heartbeats, so deceptive are her responses to men, seems to desire Willie; they sing about sharing the nights, then, at the end of the movie, Modesty leads into a reprise of the song: "You know, really we should've"; Willie replies "It's sort of less common this way," shying away from a sexual relationship with Modesty. They both use their sexual partners with the same lack of regard: Nicole asks Willie: "Where did you go that day in Rome"; immediately afterwards Hagan asks Modesty: "Where did you go that day in Paris?" Modesty, like Eve, the perfect mistress, denies she has a soul, treating her men like men treat women. Sexual contact, for both of them, might involve a denial of the respect they have for each other. When Gabriel's boat returns to his island stronghold for the last time, with Willie and Modesty prisoners on board, she joins in the boatman's song, but her voice fades away on the words "La Vita"; singing of life makes her realise what death will be — a very beautiful moment which derives added poignancy from the life that Modesty has led: the world of *Modesty Blaise* is the world of the currently fashionable and expensive — clothes (Modesty's weird costume — "How did you get it on?" Hagan asks bewildered; Modesty does not know — is hardly any tighter than the trousers Willie zips himself into), the new movie exoticism of the wealthy camp (which is contrasted with the old movie exoticism — Arab Sheik), op art, loveless sex (Mrs. Fothergill and her boys represent an extension of the attitude toward both sex and violence that Modesty displays, an attitude which exists in all of us: witness the collective fantasies now being projected on the cinema screens — the Bond cult), cars, speedboats, yachts: the trappings of escape in the affluent society. Modesty herself is a perfect consumer, though her gaiety does transform her into a positive force, a force for life, in the context established by the film. Her almost magical quick changes of costume fascinate both her and Hagan, giving a childish pleasure that is part of the world of fantasy, of the strip-cartoon, or of the cinema: the world of the dream, in which the reality principle no longer operates. At one point Losey reminds us of the way in

154

which the cinema can fake anything: Modesty aims an arrow at a guard, using a bow made up from Willie's belt; the arrow sails away past the guard, who is shot by another arrow fired in from off-camera. Throughout Losey strips bare the fantasy of the genre, breaking suspense; the movie's high camp style parodies the attempt to give a deeper meaning that so often occurs in such movies (Gabriel's mother-fixation neatly expresses an attitude both to over-glib psycho-analytical interpretations of behaviour and to the way in which such interpretations are often built into the dialogue of a picture in an attempt to lend it significance and respectability). At the same time, the movie parodies visual symbols from past Losey works — the fish in the drink, reminiscent of *Eve*; the Frink-like sculpture near the radar scanner on Gabriel's hideout *(The Damned)* — as if Losey were implying that the necessity of working in the genre of melodrama had imposed on him the need to use a certain kind of symbolism and visual style as the only means by which he was able to communicate what he desired to communicate. Gabriel, threatening Modesty, states: "Your Mr. Garvin is going to help us, otherwise . . . Oh, no, I can't say it, it's pure melodrama." "I'm the villain of the piece, and I have to condemn you to death," Gabriel tells Modesty after their arrival at his head-quarters; "But I'm the heroine, don't I get away?" she asks. "Perhaps," he replies, "Convey Mr. Garvin to the tower, and take Modesty to the cell I have prepared for her." In the cell, Modesty finds the key marked "Perhaps", which leads her to the tradi-tional temptation of the genre, to join with Gabriel — "We share the diamonds, and you eliminate Garvin. I'll eliminate Mrs. Fothergill" — a temptation which she, following the convention, rejects, settling, instead, for an attempted escape, and a burlesque last-minute rescue; the plot is so conventional that Losey destroys any semblance of normal narrative structure as irrelevant: Gabriel cables Pacco, his Amsterdam agent: "If the girl is alive tomorrow night, you won't be"; McWhirter comments: "Pacco will understand"; Gabriel replies: "I suppose so. He reads the comic strips." Yet even the conventional, the violent, can give rise to the lyrical: Nicole's flight from her assassins in the Old Market is a moment of strange beauty, as is the carefully choreographed knife fight which follows her murder; both occur as a result of Pacco's knowledge of the comic strips.

Modesty Blaise may seem rather insubstantial when compared with major Losey works such as *Blind Date*, *Eve*, *The Criminal*, *The Damned*, *King and Country*, but this lack of substance is to some extent more apparent than real, the result of its lack of formal narrative structure; its range of mood, of effect, of reference, make it a work which grows richer and more complex on repeated viewings.

19. Accident

"IN MANY ways, stylistically, I think it's different . . . It's about how characters in their lives settle down, and they stay settled all their lives, then something may happen that suddenly jumps them out of it, and they leap ahead or leap backwards, suddenly and without any warning. It is also about a group of people who, from the point of view of knowledge, not just a smattering of knowledge, but a fairly profound knowledge of all sorts of aspects of life from morality and ethics and philosophy through physics and mathematics and psychology, still don't really know what to do with it, still don't have many answers. They live in a kind of backwater, and then an accident occurs, and the accident may be a catastrophe, it may be a death — which in this case it is — but there are accidents happening all the time, which we all have to overcome.

Because, at a certain moment, depending on how you feel, what your courage is, what the situation is, what your character is, you either say or don't say, or do or don't do something which may have extraordinary effect on somebody else's life, or on your own, in terms of what you become, what you don't become, the course your life takes. It's certainly not a Pollyanna story, but it will have a good deal of humour, and it has a positive ending in the sense that the characters who are involved, and in particular the Dirk Bogarde character will live the rest of his life in memory of the particular things the film deals with — a changed man, a deeply changed man, with things in himself which he undoubtedly will never share with anybody else. And this is true of certain other characters in it too. I don't believe it will be considered sordid, I don't believe it will be considered particularly sensational. I think it may be a little tough to view. I think it will be entertainment by my definition, which is simply anything that's strong enough to interest you and hold you and to be purgative in terms of its effect, and to precipitate thinking. In that sense, I'm sure it will be. But that it may be difficult to take for some people, I also expect and hope."

Joseph Losey (J.D.L.)

It would be easy to praise *Accident* for its obvious virtues — Pinter's dialogue, or Gerry Fisher's sensitive colour photography, for example, or the acting, which is exceptional by any standards, even those set in previous Losey movies (though I, for one, have never been quite one hundred percent satisfied with Dirk Bogarde's previous roles for Losey — the great Losey performances for me have been David Wayne as M, Leo McKern as Stanford, Michael Redgrave as David Graham, Patrick Magee as Barrows, Stanley Baker in his three Losey movies — Dirk Bogarde as Stephen gives a perfect performance, one which has never been surpassed by any actor working for Losey, and one which deserves to win every acting award it is possible to win), but that would be to underestimate the movie. With *Accident*, Losey has carried his exploration of the tensions arising from the three-way conflict between man's emotional desires and needs, his legacy of guilt from the morality of the past, and his responsibility towards his fellow human beings, a stage further. Whereas in *Eve* the basic unifying pattern was the love-hatred of Tyvian and Eve, which had, as a counterpoint, the joking hostility of McCormick and Anna Maria, the basic unifying pattern of *Accident* is the less intense attraction-repulsion experienced by all the characters in their relationships; at one point, the four characters most involved in this struggle, Stephen, Charley, William and Anna, are seen on a tennis-court, enclosed by wire; outside sits Rosalind, whose security is threatened by the outcome of this struggle. The struggle is manifest in the feelings of Stephen for Charley, Anna, William, and vice versa; of Charley and Anna, William and Anna, even of Stephen towards the concept of aristocracy, and towards William and Anna as aristocrats rather than as people. "All aristocrats were made to be killed," Stephen tells William, who replies: "Of course. They're immortal" — the line lives on, even if the individual dies. Later in the movie, Stephen asks William: "Isn't it true that every aristocrat wants to die?" — perhaps to obtain a heroic immortality? — and William, suddenly maturely serious (earlier, talking about his lack of friends, his seriousness had been less mature) replies: "I don't." They are about to play in a game which seems a brutal and violent cross between the Eton wall-game and rugby — a kind of masculine sex-ritual, with strong suggestions of physical sexuality — in the hall of William's father's 'stately home'. "What do I do in goal?" Stephen asks: "Defend it," William replies, giving expression to the underlying principle of aristocratic and heroic virtue;

Hawks's John T. Chance could not have been more succinct. Stephen asks if he could not watch; no, he is told, because he is a house-guest: "Only the old men watch. And the ladies."

William has consistently taunted Stephen with his age; when they are discussing Anna, he says: "You're not past it, are you? Already?"; later he says: "I thought forty was the prime of life." At forty, Stephen is in a stage of transition; the heroic dreams of youth have been forgotten in his comfortably happy marriage to Rosalind; just as Anna and William evoke memories of the youth that has gone and cannot be recaptured — lazy, idyllic afternoons punting — so William and the TV don Charley present images of a kind of heroic success; of Charley, Stephen says: "He is more successful than me because he talks on television". Rosalind jokingly comments: "He suits the medium"; to which Stephen replies with a certain bitterness, upsetting Rosalind: "You mean that I don't suit the medium." Similarly, the Provost, extolling how "good" William is (at games, but the implication is that prowess at games, because heroic, is the supreme form of prowess), asks Stephen: "How about you, Stephen? Were you any good?" A few moments later, Stephen, remembering what was "good" about his youth, tells the Provost: "I saw Francesca when I was in London"; the Provost looks puzzled, so Stephen adds: "Your daughter." "Ah," says the Provost, suddenly remembering, "Please give her my love when you see her again."

The nervous, sneaky looks the Provost gives Stephen during the conversation remind one of one of the movie's central themes: responsibility, to one's friends, and as a parent: Francesca, who is little more than the shell of a woman, though she exudes a hysteric femininity of some fascination, is the Provost's daughter; Stephen, as a tutor, is "in loco parentis" vis-à-vis his pupils; Rosalind is pregnant, and Stephen, desiring Anna, ignores a telephone call which would have told him of the premature birth of his third child. Though Stephen's desire to mix two worlds, his two personalities — as don, and as husband and father — leads to a disaster, an accident, Stephen, unlike Charley (or perhaps the Provost) is unwilling to run the risk of killing his children's hopes: the forlorn, uncomprehending image of Charley's son, perched on a window-sill throughout Stephen's confrontation with Charley's wife, Laura, is comment enough on Charley's failure. Charley and the Provost, with his arid intellectuality (his cheap jokes about American universities are a sign of his total sterility) represent the two opposed extremes of irresponsibility, one destructive, the other sterile, towards which Stephen might be drawn. As a person, Stephen has affinities with the characters of both Charley and the Provost, but he is finally able to avoid both extremes, and stay *alive* spiritually and emotionally, because he is Stephen. The final image of Stephen in the movie, with his child who has fallen over, and with the sound of the accident ever-present in his consciousness, establish clearly that he has finally accepted his responsibility; if anything, he may have become slightly over-concerned. Yet he has been guilty of deep failures of responsibility: to William, towards whom he behaved as a rival rather than as a tutor (this becomes finally clear in the "game"); to Francesca, whom he used, in an attempt to revive the lost sexuality of his youth, an attempt which failed because, knowing he was trying to use her, he was guilty before the act, and because Francesca, despite her pathetic protestations of happiness, and her poignant references to the past, had retreated into an existence as emotionally sterile as her father's; to Anna, on whom he projected his own desires, to recapture his lost youth, and to be a hero: if Anna is a princess, her lover in the tale must be a prince of sorts; in real life, though, there is nothing heroic about becoming a prince by seducing one of one's students, particularly one who is suffering from intense shock. Though there is something beautiful

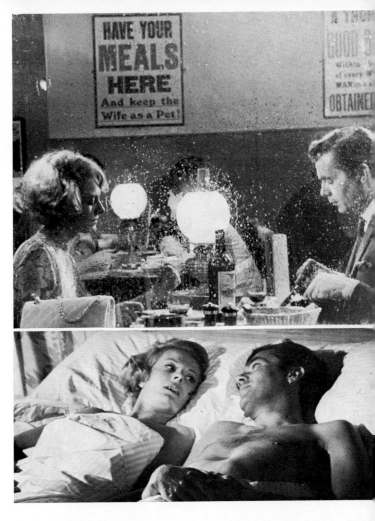

ACCIDENT. The scenes between Francesca (Delphine Seyrig) and Stephen (Dirk Bogarde), which in terms of theme and psychological motivation represent an extremely callous incident, took on as they were shot a kind of dreamlike inevitability and poignancy – evocative of something past and lost – indicative of Losey's intense compassion for a certain kind of waste.

ACCIDENT: Stephen (Dirk Bogarde) and Anna (Jacqueline Sassard). Throughout the movie, their relationship is one of attraction and repulsion.

ACCIDENT. Below left: Charlie (Stanley Baker) and Anna provide a surprise for Stephen when he returns home. Below right: the violence beneath the civilised exterior. Stephen and William (Michael York) during the game.

about the fairy-tale concept of a princess — one of the movie's most beautiful moments is when Stephen's little daughter interrupts her parents' bantering conversation about Anna to insist: "She *is* a princess" — it is base of Stephen to desire Anna *because* she is a princess; he is denying — as do Charley, and even William, both of whom project their image of their own desires and needs on to her — her individual identity, just as he does that of Francesca. However, Stephen and Anna, unlike Stephen and Francesca, are able to transcend the struggle, go beyond the loveless sexual phantasy — which, though it may be intensely exciting, is, by itself, essentially uncreative — to some kind of genuine communication. This is something Charley, or, say, the characters in *The Servant*, can never attain to. Thus, though they are drained next morning, Stephen and Anna are both capable of realising that they have no kind of future together, that their most important needs must carry them apart. "There's nothing to keep her here," Stephen tells Charley, who is trying, half begging, half bullying, to persuade Anna to stay.

In an imperfect world, Stephen, and possibly Anna, who can learn something of responsibility by experiencing and living through their desires, accepting, too, guilt for their failures of responsibility and living with it, are positive figures compared with Francesca, the Provost, Charley (who is clearly incapable of any kind of self-control, confessing at one point to Stephen about his obsession with Anna: "I don't know what to do, you see. I can't have enough of her"), or Laura, who is forced by her marital crisis into a schizoid gardening-compulsion. Stephen's confrontation with Laura is cut into the scene where Stephen tells Rosalind about Charley's split with Laura and passion for Anna; this is not merely because Charley and Laura's marriage is, at this point, crucially relevant to both the past and future of Stephen and Rosalind, but also because the two events are inseparably fused in Stephen's consciousness: the major narrative of the movie is told in a kind of flashback, filtered through Stephen's consciousness, which comes after the accident, and before Stephen's seduction of Anna. In the seduction, Stephen finally rids himself of the blocks that have been oppressing him throughout the movie; perhaps Anna does too; we are less clear what the effects of the cumulative experience conveyed by the movie are on her precisely because we see the events of the movie filtered through *Stephen's* consciousness, not hers: there is nothing shown, apart from the movie's opening and closing shots, which are from the audience's viewpoint, that could not have been experienced, or, as in the case of Charley alone in his rooms in College, imagined by Stephen. Whilst telling Rosalind about Charley, Laura and Anna, Stephen casually mentions that he had dinner in London with Francesca: "You remember Francesca?" he asks; Rosalind's reply is a slightly gasped: "Yes." Then she bursts out with abuse for Charley, Anna, Laura even, but has the strength and self-control not to say anything likely to damage her relationship with Stephen.

The bland, inconsequential dialogue of most of the movie does more than suggest the hyper-civilised, hyper-intellectual atmosphere of Oxford as filtered through Stephen's highly intellectual consciousness. Losey uses Pinter much as Resnais (whom Losey has described to me as "virtually the only director I can learn from" has used Robbe-Grillet and the literary tradition being established by the "new novelists": to create a *surface*, a set of sense data, or percepts, which can be examined. Such a surface establishes its own reality, or truth: William's objective description of the scene in the garden — "Rosalind's lying down. Stephen's weeding the garden . . ." — has a validity, and a beauty, of its own. So, too, does Charley's "probing" beneath the surface: "Stephen is having an affair with a girl at Oxford . . ." If William is a "new novelist", Charley is a teller of melodramatic, commercially successful stories; yet Charley's story is a confession of what he actually *is* doing, and a forecast of what Stephen might do (it visibly disturbs Stephen, and Rosalind's subsequent behaviour that day shows that even she, the image of maternal dependability, is upset): the objective "new novel" has become the story, or phantasy, the melodrama truth. But the melodrama is not the whole truth, because Charley's guilt forces him to cast Stephen in the role he himself is actually playing.

In this film, Losey's visual style, often unfairly criticised as baroque, or over-ornate, is remarkably chaste, depicting objects as objects rather than as symbols; thus it accurately reflects the consciousness of the philosopher Stephen. His stylised editing admirably evokes the fleeting nature of impressions, memories (Losey even cuts sound with visual at certain points, for example in the punt). The movie's opening shot — the very slightest movement forward — carries us through the gates, towards the house and Stephen's unifying consciousness; its closing shot — the slightest movement back away from the house — carries us away from Stephen, but the soundtrack, repeating the sound of the accident, maintains our link with his consciousness: "accidents", past or future, are potentially an ever-present factor in human experience, yet they need not *determine* human behaviour.

The truth that *Accident* embodies is a synthesis of the truth contained in the stories of both Charley and William. It is one which could only have been expressed by a director of intense intellectual rigour; one who is, too, a master of his craft, working with collaborators whose mastery of their crafts equals his own.

Filmography

Short films

PETE ROLEUM AND HIS COUSINS. U.S.A. 1939. *Prod, dir, sc:* Joseph Losey. Technicolor. *mus:* Hanns Eisler.

A CHILD WENT FORTH. U.S.A. 1940-41. Made for New York University. *Dir, sc:* Joseph Losey. *ph:* John Ferno. *mus:* Hanns Eisler.

YOUTH GETS A BREAK. U.S.A. 1940-41. Made for the National Youth Administration. *Dir, sc:* Joseph Losey. *ph:* Willard van Dyke, Ralph Steiner, John Ferno.

A GUN IN HIS HAND. U.S.A. 1945. A "Crime Does Not Pay" subject, released by Metro-Goldwyn-Mayer. *Dir:* Joseph Losey. *sc:* Charles F. Royal, from a story by Richard Landau. *ed:* Harry Kromer. *mus:* Max Terr.

Feature films

THE BOY WITH GREEN HAIR. U.S.A. 1948. Released by R.K.O. Radio. *Exec prod:* Dore Schary. *prod:* Adrian Scott, then Stephen Ames. *dir:* Joseph Losey. *sc:* Ben Barzman and Alfred Lewis Levitt, from a short story by Betsy Beaton. *ph:* George Barnes (Technicolor). *art dir:* Albert S. D'Agostino and Ralph Berger. *ed:* Frank Doyle. *mus:* Leigh Harline. 82 mins.

CAST: Pat O'Brien *(Gramp);* Robert Ryan *(Dr. Evans);* Barbara Hale *(Miss Brand);* Dean Stockwell *(Peter);* Richard Lyon *(Michael);* Walter Catlett *("The King");* Samuel S. Hinds *(Dr. Knudson);* Regis Toomey *(Mr. Davis);* Charles Meredith *(Mr. Piper);* David Clarke *(Barber);* Billy Sheffield *(Red);* John Calkins *(Danny);* Teddy Infuhr *(Timmy);* Dwayne Hickman *(Joey);* Eilene Janssen *(Peggy);* Curtis Jackson *(Classmate);* Charles Arnt *(Mr. Hammond).*

Shot in 36 days.

THE LAWLESS (British title, **THE DIVIDING LINE**). U.S.A. 1949. A Pine-Thomas production, released by Paramount. *Prod:* William H. Pine and William C. Thomas. *dir:* Joseph Losey. *sc:* Geoffrey Homes (pseudonym of Daniel Mainwaring), from his novel *The Voice of Stephen Wilder*. *ph:* Roy Hunt. *prod layout:* John Hubley. *art dir:* Lewis H. Creber. *ed:* Howard Smith. *mus:* Mahlon Merrick. 83 mins.

CAST: Macdonald Carey *(Larry Wilder);* Gail Russell *(Sunny Garcia);* John Sands *(Joe Ferguson);* Lee Patrick *(Jan Dawson);* Lalo Rios *(Paul Rodriguez);* Maurice Jara *(Lopo Chavez);* Walter Reed *(Jim Wilson);* Guy Anderson *(Jonas Creel);* Argentina Brunetti *(Mrs. Rodriguez);* William Edmunds *(Mr. Jensen);* Martha Hyer *(Caroline Tyler);* Frank Fenton *(Mr. Prentiss);* Paul Harvey *(Chief of State Police);* Ian MacDonald *(Al Peters);* Julia Faye *(Mrs. Jensen);* Pedro de Cordoba *(Mr. Garcia).*

Shot in 23 days.

THE PROWLER. U.S.A. 1950. A Horizon Pictures production, released by United Artists. *Prod:* S. P. Eagle (Sam Spiegel). *dir:* Joseph Losey. *asst dir:* Robert Aldrich. *sc:* Dalton Trumbo, then Hugo Butler, from an original story by Robert Thoeren and Hans Wilhelm. *ph:* Arthur Miller. *prod layout:* John Hubley. *art dir:* Boris Leven. *set dec:* Jacques Mapes. *ed:* Paul Weatherwax. *mus:* Lyn Murray. 91 mins.

CAST: Van Heflin *(Webb Garwood);* Evelyn Keyes *(Susan Gilvray);* John Maxwell *(Bud Crocker);* Katherine Warren *(Mrs. Crocker);* Emerson Treacy *(William Gilvray);* Madge Blake *(Martha Gilvray);* Wheaton Chambers *(Dr. James);* Robert Osterloh *(Coroner);* Sherry Hall *(John Gilvray);* Louise Lorimer *(Motel Manager).*

Shot in 17 days.

M. U.S.A. 1950. Released by Columbia. *Prod:* Seymour and Harold Nebenzal. *dir:* Joseph Losey. *asst dir:* Robert Aldrich.

sc: Norman Reilly Raine and Leo Katcher. *add dia:* Waldo Salt. *ph:* Ernest Lazslo. *prod layout:* John Hubley. *art dir:* Martin Obzina. *set dec:* Ray Robinson. *ed:* Edward Mann. *mus:* Michel Michelet. 88 mins.

CAST: David Wayne *("M"); * Howard da Silva *(Carney); * Luther Adler *(Langley); * Martin Gabel *(Marshall); * Steve Brodie *(Lt. Becker); * Raymond Burr *(Pottsy); * Glenn Anders *(Riggert); * Karen Morley *(Mrs. Coster); * Norman Lloyd *(Sutro); * John Miljan *(Blind Vendor); * Walter Burke *(MacMahan); * Roy Engel *(Regan); * Benny Burt *(Jansen); * Lennie Bremen *(Lemke); * Jim Backus *(Mayor); * Janine Perreau *(Little girl); * Robin Fletcher *(Elsie Coster); * Bernard Szolk *(Watchman); * Jorja Curtright *(Mrs. Stewart).*

Shot in 20 days.

THE BIG NIGHT. U.S.A. 1951. A Philip A. Waxman production, released by United Artists. *Prod:* Philip A. Waxman. *dir:* Joseph Losey. *asst dir:* Ivan Volkman. *sc:* Hugo Butler, then Ring Lardner Jr. and Joseph Losey, from the novel *The Dreadful Summit* by Stanley Ellin. *ph:* Hal Mohr. *art dir:* Nicholas Remisoff. *ed:* Edward Mann. *mus:* Lyn Murray. 71 mins. (U.K.); 75 mins. (U.S.A.).

CAST: John Barrymore Jr. *(George La Main); * Preston Foster *(Andy La Main); * Howland Chamberlain *(Flanagan); * Howard St. John *(Al Judge); * Philip Bourneuf *(Dr. Lloyd Cooper); * Emile Meyer *(Peckinpaugh); * Dorothy Comingore *(Julie Rostina); * Joan Lorring *(Marion Rostina); * Mauri Lynn *(Singer).*

Shot in 24 days.

STRANGER ON THE PROWL (also known as **ENCOUNTER**). (Italian title: IMBARCO A MEZZANOTE; French title: UN HOMME A DETRUIRE). Filmed in Italy, 1951. A Conzorcio Produttori Cinematographicafici Tirrenia and Riviera Films production, released by United Artists (Italy: Generalcine). *Prod, dir:*

Joseph Losey (under the name of Andrea Forzano) *sc:* Ben Barzman, from a short story by Noël Calef, *La Bouteille de Lait. ph:* Henri Alekan. *ed:* Thelma Connell. *mus:* G. C. Sonzogno. 180 mins. originally; subsequently 100 mins. and 80 mins.

CAST: Paul Muni *(The Man);* Joan Lorring *(Angela);* Vittorio Manunta *(Giacomo);* Luisa Rossi *(Giacomo's Mother);* Aldo Silvani *(Peroni);* Arnold Foa *(The Inspector);* Alfred Varelli *(Policeman);* Elena Manson *(Dairymaid);* Fausta Maezzunchelli, Cesare Trapani, Enrico Glori, Fianco Balducci, Léon Lenoir, Linda Sini.

Shot in 86 days.

THE SLEEPING TIGER. U.K. 1954. An Insignia Films production, released by Anglo-Amalgamated. *Prod:* Victor Hanbury. *dir:* Joseph Losey (credited to Victor Hanbury). *asst dir:* Denis Johnson. *sc:* Harold Buchman and Carl Foreman, from the novel by Maurice Moisewisch. *ph:* Harry Waxman. *art dir:* John Stoll. *ed:* Reginald Mills. *mus:* Malcolm Arnold. 89 mins.

CAST: Dirk Bogarde *(Frank Clements);* Alexis Smith *(Glenda Esmond);* Alexander Knox *(Dr. Clive Esmond);* Hugh Griffith *(Inspector Simmons);* Patricia McCarron *(Sally);* Maxine Audley *(Carol);* Glyn Houston *(Bailey);* Harry Towb *(Harry);* Russell Waters *(Manager);* Billie Whitelaw *(Receptionist);* Fred Griffiths *(Taxi Driver);* Esma Cannon *(Window Cleaner).*

A MAN ON THE BEACH. U.K. 1955. A Hammer Films production, released by Exclusive. *Prod:* Anthony Hinds. *dir:* Joseph Losey. *sc:* Jimmy Sangster, from the novel *Chance at the Wheel* by Victor Canning. *ph:* Wilkie Cooper (Cinepanorama, Eastmancolor) *prod layout:* Richard MacDonald. *ed:* Henry Richardson. *mus:* John Hotchkis. 29 mins.

CAST: Donald Wolfit *(Carter);* Michael Medwin *(Max);* Michael Ripper *(Chauffeur);* Alex de Gallier *(Casino Manager);* Edward Forsyth *(Clement);* Kirk S. Siegenburg *(Little Boy);*

Shandre Walden *(Little Girl)*.

THE INTIMATE STRANGER (American title, **A FINGER OF GUILT**). U.K. 1955. An Anglo Guild production, released by Anglo-Amalgamated. *Prod:* Alec Snowden. *dir:* Joseph Losey (under the name Joseph Walton). *sc:* Howard Koch (under the name Peter Howard). *ph:* Geoffrey Muller. *prod layout:* Richard MacDonald. *mus:* Trevor Duncan. 89 mins.

CAST: Richard Basehart *(Reggie Wilson);* Mary Murphy *(Evelyn Stewart);* Constance Cummings *(Kay Wallace);* Roger Livesey *(Ben Case);* Mervyn Johns *(Ernest Chaple);* Faith Brook *(Lesley Wilson);* Vernon Greeves *(George Mearns);* Andre Mikhelson; Basil Dignam, Grace Denbeigh Russell; Frederic Steger; Wilfred Downing; Edna Lander; Jack Stewart.

TIME WITHOUT PITY. U.K. 1956. A Harlequin production, released by Eros Films. *Exec prod:* Leon Clore. *prod:* John Arnold and Anthony Simmons. *dir:* Joseph Losey. *sc:* Ben Barzman, from a play by Emlyn Williams. *ph:* Freddie Francis. *prod layout:* Richard MacDonald. *prod designer:* Reece Pemberton. *art dir:* Bernard Sarron. *ed:* Alan Osbiston. *mus:* Tristram Cary. 88 mins.

CAST: Michael Redgrave *(David Graham);* Ann Todd *(Honor Stanford);* Leo McKern *(Robert Stanford);* Peter Cushing *(Jeremy Clayton);* Alec McCowen *(Alec Graham);* Renee Huston *(Mrs. Harker);* Paul Daneman *(Brian Stanford);* Lois Maxwell *(Vicky Harker);* Richard Wordsworth *(Maxwell);* George Devine *(Barnes);* Joan Plowright *(Agnes Cole);* Ernest Clarke *(Under Secretary);* Peter Copley *(Padre);* Hugh Moxey *(Prison Governor);* Julian Somers *(First warder);* John Chandos *(First journalist);* Dickie Henderson Jr. *(Comedian)*.

THE GYPSY AND THE GENTLEMAN. U.K. 1957. Released by Rank. *Exec prod:* Earl St. John. *prod:* Maurice Cowan. *dir:* Joseph Losey. *asst dir:* Robert Asher. *sc:* Janet Green, from the novel *Darkness, I Leave You* by Nina Warner Hooke. *ph:* Jack Hildyard

(Eastmancolor). *prod layout:* Richard MacDonald and Ralph Brinton. *art dir:* Ralph Brinton. *costumes:* Julie Harris. *historical advisor:* Vyvyan Holland. *ed:* Reginald Beck. *mus:* Hans May. 107 mins.

CAST: Melina Mercouri *(Belle);* Keith Michell *(Paul Deverill);* Patrick McGoohan *(Jess);* June Laverick *(Sarah Deverill);* Lyndon Brook *(John);* Flora Robson *(Mrs. Haggard);* Clare Austin *(Vanessa);* Helen Haye *(Lady Ayrton);* Newton Blick *(Ruddock);* Mervyn Johns *(Brook);* John Salew *(Duffin);* Edna Morris *(Mrs. Piggot);* Gladys Boot *(Mrs. Mortimer);* Catherine Feller *(Hattie);* Laurence Naismith *(Forrester);* David Hart *(Will);* Louis Aquilina *(Coco);* Nigel Green *(Game Pup);* Laurence Taylor *(Cropped Harry).*

BLIND DATE (American title, **CHANCE MEETING**). U.K. 1959. An Independent Artists-Julian Wintle & Leslie Parkyn production for Sidney Box, released by Rank. *Prod:* David Deutsch. *dir:* Joseph Losey. *sc:* Ben Barzman and Millard Lampell, from the novel by Leigh Howard. *ph:* Christopher Challis. *prod layout:* Richard MacDonald. *art dir:* Edward Carrick. *ed:* Reginald Mills. *mus:* Richard Rodney Bennett. 95 mins.

CAST: Hardy Kruger *(Jan van Rooyen);* Stanley Baker *(Inspector Morgan);* Micheline Presle *(Jacqueline Cousteau);* Robert Flemyng *(Sir Brian Lewis);* Gordon Jackson *(Police Sergeant);* John van Eyssen *(Westover);* Jack MacGowran *(Postman);* George Roubicek *(Police Constable);* Redmond Phillips *(Police Doctor).*

THE CRIMINAL (American title, **THE CONCRETE JUNGLE**). U.K. 1960. A Nat Cohen and Stuart Levy — Merton Park Studios production, released by Anglo Amalgamated. *Prod:* Jack Greenwood. *dir:* Joseph Losey. *sc:* Alun Owen and Jimmy Sangster. *ph:* Robert Krasker. *prod layout:* Richard Macdonald. *art dir:* Scott MacGregor. *mus:* Johnny Dankworth. 97 mins.

CAST: Stanley Baker *(Johnny Bannion);* Sam Wanamaker

(Mike Carter); Gregoire Aslan *(Frank Saffron);* Margit Saad *(Suzanne);* Jill Bennett *(Maggie);* Rupert Davies *(Mr. Edwards);* Laurence Naismith *(Mr. Town);* John van Eyssen *(Formby);* Noel Willman *(Prison Governor);* Derek Francis *(Priest);* Redmond Phillips *(Prison Doctor);* Kenneth J. Warren *(Clobber);* Patrick Magee *(Chief Warder);* Kenneth Cope *(Kelly);* Patrick Wymark *(Sol);* Jack Rodney *(Scout);* John Molloy *(Snipe);* Brian Phelan *(Pauly Larkin);* Paul Stassino *(Alfredo Fanucci);* Jerold Wells *(Warder Brown);* Tom Bell *(Flynn);* Neil McCarthy *(O'Hara);* Keith Smith *(Hanson);* Nigel Green *(Ted);* Tom Gerard *(Quantock);* Larry Taylor *(Chas);* Murray Melvin *(Antlers).*

THE DAMNED (American title, **THESE ARE THE DAMNED**). U.K. 1961. A Hammer Films production, released by Columbia. *Exec prod:* Michael Carreras. *prod:* Anthony Nelson Keys and Anthony Hinds. *dir:* Joseph Losey. *asst dir:* John Peverall. *sc:* Evan Jones, from the novel *The Children of Light* by H. L. Lawrence. *ph:* Arthur Grant (Cinemascope). *prod layout:* Richard MacDonald. *prod design:* Bernard Robinson. *art dir:* Don Mingaye. *supervising ed:* James Needs. *ed:* Reginald Mills. *mus:* James Bernard. 87 mins.

CAST: Macdonald Carey *(Simon Wells);* Shirley Anne Field *(Joan);* Viveca Lindfors *(Freya);* Alexander Knox *(Bernard);* Oliver Reed *(King);* Walter Gotell *(Major Holland);* James Villiers *(Captain Gregory);* Thomas Kempinski *(Ted);* Kenneth Cope *(Sid);* Brian Oulton *(Mr. Dingle);* Barbara Everest *(Miss Lamont);* Alan McClelland *(Mr. Stuart);* James Maxwell *(Mr. Talbot);* Rachel Clay *(Victoria);* Caroline Sheldon *(Elizabeth);* Rebecca Dignam *(Anne);* Siobhan Taylor *(Mary);* Nicholas Clay *(Richard);* Kit Williams *(Henry);* Christopher Witty *(William);* David Palmer *(George);* John Thompson *(Charles).*

EVE. Italy. 1961-2. A Paris-Films Productions — Interopa Films production. *Prod:* Robert and Raymond Hakim. *dir:* Joseph Losey.

sc: Evan Jones and Hugo Butler, from a novel by James Hadley Chase. *ph:* Gianni Di Venanzo. *prod layout and art dir:* Richard MacDonald and Luigi Scaccianoce. *ed:* Reginald Beck and Franca Silva. *mus:* Michel Legrand. 120 mins.

CAST: Jeanne Moreau *(Eve Olivier);* Stanley Baker *(Tyvian Jones);* Virna Lisi *(Francesca);* Giorgio Albertazzi *(Branco Malloni);* Nona Medici *(Anna Maria);* Francesco Rissone *(Pieri);* James Villiers *(Alan McCormick);* Alex Revides *(The Greek);* Lisa Gastoni; Ricardo Garrone.

THE SERVANT. U.K. 1963. A Springbok-Elstree production, released by Warner-Pathe. *prod:* Joseph Losey and Norman Priggen. *dir:* Joseph Losey. *sc:* Harold Pinter, from the novel by Robin Maugham. *ph:* Douglas Slocombe. *prod designer:* Richard MacDonald. *art dir:* Ted Clements. *ed:* Reginald Mills. *mus:* John Dankworth. 115 mins.

CAST: Dirk Bogarde *(Barrett);* Sarah Miles *(Vera);* Wendy Craig *(Susan);* James Fox *(Tony);* Catherine Lacey *(Lady Mountset);* Richard Vernon *(Lord Mountset);* Ann Firbank *(Society Woman);* Doris Knox *(Older Woman);* Patrick Magee *(Bishop);* Jill Melford *(Younger Woman);* Alun Owen *(Curate);* Harold Pinter *(Society Man);* Derek Tansley *(Head Waiter);* Brian Phelan *(Man in Pub);* Hazel Terry *(Woman in Bedroom);* Philippa Hare *(Girl in Bedroom);* Dorothy Bromily *(Girl in phone box);* Alison Seebohm *(Girl in Pub);* Chris Williams *(Cashier in coffee bar);* Gerry Dugan *(Waiter).*

KING AND COUNTRY. U.K. 1964. A B.H.E. production, released by Warner-Pathe. *Exec prod:* Daniel M. Angel. *prod:* Joseph Losey and Normal Priggen. *assoc prod:* Richard Goodwin. *dir:* Joseph Losey. *asst dir:* Scott Wodehouse. *sc:* Evan Jones, from the play by John Wilson based on a story by James Lansdale Hodson. *ph:* Denys Coop. *prod designer:* Richard MacDonald. *art dir:* Peter Mullins. *ed:* Reginald Mills. *mus:* Larry Adler. 86 mins.

CAST: Dirk Bogarde *(Captain Hargreaves);* Tom Courtenay *(Private Hamp);* Leo McKern *(Captain O'Sullivan);* Barry Foster *(Lt. Webb);* James Villiers *(Captain Midgley);* Peter Copley *(Colonel);* Barry Justice *(Lt. Prescott);* Vivian Matalon *(Padre);* Jeremy Spenser *(Sparrow);* James Hunter *(Sykes);* David Cook *(Wilson);* Larry Taylor *(Sergeant-Major);* Jonah Seymour *(Corporal M.P.);* Keith Buckley *(Corporal of the Guard);* Richard Arthure *(Guard 'Charlie');* Derek Partridge *(Captain at Court Martial);* Raymond Brody, Terry Palmer, Dan Cornwall *(Soldiers).*

MODESTY BLAISE. U.K. 1966. A Modesty Blaise Ltd. production, released by Twentieth Century-Fox. *Prod:* Joseph Janni. *assoc prod:* Norman Priggen and Michael Birkett. *dir:* Joseph Losey. *asst dir:* Gavrik Losey and Claude Watson. *sc:* Evan Jones, based on the comic strip created by Peter O'Donnell and Jim Holdaway. *ph:* Jack Hildyard (Technicolor). *additional ph:* Dave Boulton. *prod designer:* Richard MacDonald. *art dir:* Jack Shampan. *costumes:* Bumble Dawson. *ed:* Reginald Beck. *mus:* John Dankworth. 119 mins.

CAST: Monica Vitti *(Modesty Blaise);* Terence Stamp *(Willie Garvin);* Dirk Bogarde *(Gabriel);* Harry Andrews *(Sir Gerald Tarrant);* Michael Craig *(Paul Hagan);* Scilla Gabel *(Melina);* Tina Marquand *(Nicole);* Clive Revill *(McWhirter* and *The Sheik);* Rosella Falk *(Mrs. Fothergill);* Joe Melia *(Crevier);* Lex Schoorel *(Walter);* Silvan *(The Great Pacco);* Jon Bluming *(Hans);* Roberto Bisacco *(Enrico);* Saro Urzi *(Basilio);* Giuseppe Pagnelli *(Friar);* Alexander Knox *(Minister);* Michael Chow *(Wang);* Marcello Turilli *(Strauss);* John Karlsen *(Oleg);* Robin Fox *(The doorbell ringer).*

ACCIDENT. U.K. 1967. A Royal Avenue Chelsea production, released by London Independent Producers (Distribution) Ltd. *Prod:* Joseph Losey and Norman Priggen. *dir:* Joseph Losey.

sc: Harold Pinter, from the novel by Nicholas Mosley. *ph:* Gerry Fisher (Eastmancolor). *art dir:* Carmen Dillon. *ed:* Reginald Beck. *mus:* John Dankworth. 105 mins.

CAST: Dirk Bogarde *(Stephen);* Stanley Baker *(Charley);* Jacqueline Sassard *(Anna);* Michael York *(William);* Vivien Merchant *(Rosalind);* Delphine Seyrig *(Francesca);* Alexander Knox *(The Provost);* Ann Firbank *(Laura);* Brian Phelan *(Police Sergeant);* Terence Rigby *(Plain-clothes Policeman);* Jane Hillary *(T.V. Receptionist);* Harold Pinter *(Mr. Bell);* Freddie Jones *(Frantic man in T.V. studio);* Jill Johnson *(Secretary);* Maxwell Findlater *(Ted);* Carole Caplin *(Clarissa);* Nicholas Mosley *(Hedges).*

Selected Bibliography

THERE are two book-length studies of Losey in French: *Losey* by Pierre Rissient in the Editions Universitaires series (1966); *Joseph Losey* by Christian Ledieu in the Cinéma d'Aujourd'hui series (1964); the latter contains some very important comments by Losey on his films. The French magazine *Image et Son* has published a complete bibliography of articles on Losey in French. This list contains material in English concerning Losey; articles marked * seem to the author to be of particular interest and importance.

A. By Losey:
 A Mirror to Life: Films and Filming, June 1959.
The Individual Eye: Encore, March-April 1961.
 The Monkey on my Back: Films and Filming, October 1963.
 10 Questions to 9 Directors, section on *The Servant, Sight and Sound* Spring 1964.

B. Interviews and Conversations with Losey and his collaborators:

Joseph Losey on The Criminal by Ian Cameron, Mark Shivas and V. F. Perkins in the joint *Granta Oxford Opinion* February 18th. 1961.

Conversations with Nicholas Ray and Joseph Losey by Penelope Houston and John Gillett in *Sight and Sound*, Autumn 1961.

Losey: Eve and The Damned (taped reply to a question), *Movie* No. 6., Jan 1963.

Isis No. 1456, on *The Servant*, Feb. 1st. 1964.

Joseph Losey and The Servant by Jacques Brunius, *Film* No. 38.

Three Designers by Roger Hudson, section on Richard MacDonald; *Sight and Sound*, Winter 1964-65.

The Secret Profession by Roger Hudson, section on Douglas Slocombe, *Sight and Sound*, Summer 1965.

Accident by John Russell Taylor, *Sight and Sound*, Autumn 1966.

Joseph Losey and the Cinema of Violence by James Leahy, *Panorama Magazine, Chicago Daily News*, Jan. 28th. 1967.

C. Reviews and Articles on Losey:

The Criminal by Richard Roud, *Sight and Sound*, Autumn 1960.

The Criminal by Peter John Dyer, *Monthly Film Bulletin*, November 1960.

The Case of Joseph Losey, paragraph in *The British Cinema*, and *The Damned*, Photo Feature, both in *Movie* No. 1., June 1962.

Joseph Losey by Andrew Sarris, *Film Culture* No. 28., Spring 1963.

Contamination by Paul Mayersberg, *Movie* No. 9., May 1963.

The Damned by Tom Milne, *Monthly Film Bulletin*, May 1963.

The Damned by Eric Rhode, *Sight and Sound*, Summer 1963.

Eve by John Russell Taylor, *Sight and Sound*, Autumn 1963.

The Servant and The Caretaker by John Russell Taylor, *Sight and Sound*, Winter 1963-64.

On Losey, articles by Jonathan Gili and Misha Donat, *Isis*, No. 1456.

The Servant by Ernest Callenbach, *Film Quarterly*, Vol. 18, No. 1, Fall 1964.

King and Country, *Monthly Film Bulletin*, Dec. 1964.

King and Country by Penelope Gilliatt, *Sight and Sound*, Winter 1964-65.

King and Country by Charles Barr, *Movie* No. 12, Spring 1965.

The Servant as Sex Thriller by T. J. Ross, *December* (Chicago).

Condemned to Silence by Jean Inobran, *Cahiers du Cinéma in English* No. 3., 1966.

Notes on an Early Losey by T. J. Ross, and *King and Country* by Stephen Gottlieb, both in *Film Culture* No. 40, Spring 1966.

Joseph Losey, or the Camera Calls by Gilles Jacob, *Sight and Sound*, Spring 1966.

Losey: Modesty and Eve (April), *Losey: Puritan Maids* (May), both by Raymond Durgnat, *Films and Filming*, 1966.

Modesty Blaise, *Monthly Film Bulletin*, June 1966.

Losey's Paper Handkerchief by Penelope Houston, *Sight and Sound*, Summer 1966.